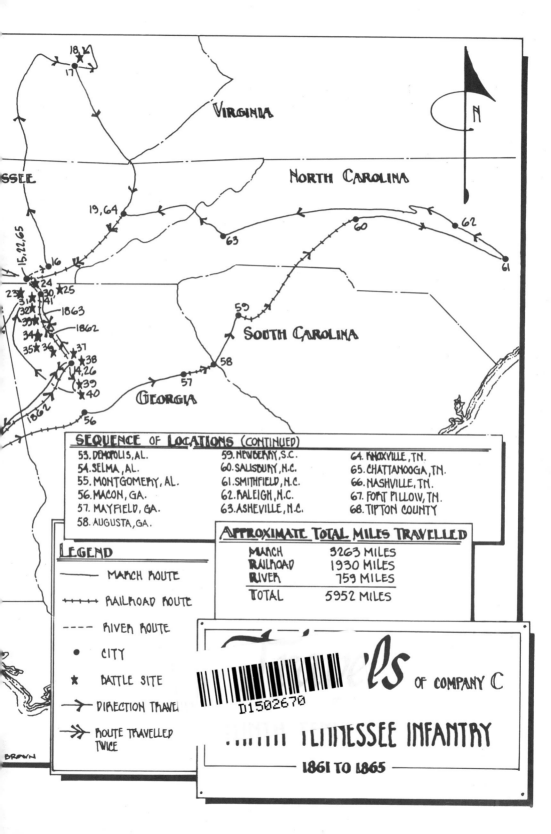

VIRGINIA

NORTH CAROLINA

SSEE

SOUTH CAROLINA

GEORGIA

N

APPROXIMATE TOTAL MILES TRAVELLED

MARCH	3263 MILES
RAILROAD	1930 MILES
RIVER	759 MILES
TOTAL	5952 MILES

LEGEND

——— MARCH ROUTE

+++++ RAILROAD ROUTE

- - - - RIVER ROUTE

• CITY

★ BATTLE SITE

→ DIRECTION TRAVEL

⇒ ROUTE TRAVELLED TWICE

BROWN

...'s OF COMPANY C

.... TENNESSEE INFANTRY

— 1861 TO 1865 —

D1502670

BAND OF BROTHERS

Company C, 9th Tennessee Infantry

by
JAMES R. FLEMING

 White Mane Publishing Company, Inc.

The acknowledgments for the illustrations used in this book are at the back of the
book.

This White Mane Publishing Company, Inc. publication was printed by:
Beidel Printing House, Inc.
63 West Burd Street
Shippensburg, PA 17257 USA

In respect for the scholarship contained herein, the acid-free paper used in this book
meets the guidelines for permanence and durability of the Committee on Production
Guidelines for Book Longevity of the Council of Library Resources.

For a complete list of available publications please write:
White Mane Publishing Company, Inc.
P.O. Box 152
Shippensburg, PA 17257-0152

Library of Congress Cataloging-in-Publication Data

Fleming, James R. (James Robert), 1956–
    Band of brothers : Company C, 9th Tennessee Infantry / by James R.
Fleming.
       p.   cm.
    Includes bibliographical references and index.
    ISBN 1-57249-003-9 (hc : alk. paper)
    1. Confederate States of America. Army. Tennessee Infantry
Regiment, 9th. Company C. 2. United States--History--Civil War,
1861–1865--Regimental histories. 3. Tennessee--History--Civil War,
1861–1865--Regimental histories. I. Title.
E579.5 9th.F538 1996
973.7'468--dc20   96-11940
                                                        CIP

PRINTED IN THE UNITED STATES OF AMERICA

We Few, We Happy Few,
We Band of Brothers

WILLIAM SHAKESPEARE
FROM KING HENRY V

DEDICATION

I originally planned on dedicating this publication to my sixty-one Confederate ancestors. I feel that the information contained herein is a tribute to their heroism, courage, stamina, religious conviction and patriotism. Instead, I would like to dedicate these chapters to the South's future generations, that they might retain the morals of those great men.

Chivalry is a precious trait. It was a way of life in the 1860s. May it become a way of life in the 1990s.

TABLE OF CONTENTS

PREFACE

To obtain the absolute, honest facts of any situation, you should refer to the primary source. The memoirs, correspondence and even obituaries within these covers were penned by active participants and thus this book is a primary source.

As the twentieth century comes to a close, the attitudes, morals and manners of the nineteenth century seem even more distant. This was our country in its infancy, forming the basis of our society today. Many pseudo-historians wrongly attempt to apply today's values to the words and actions of the Confederate soldier. In order to fully understand the nineteenth-century Southerner, you must first envision his character—his background—the morals and manners of his peers and the economic and moral situation of his nation as a whole. Then, and only then, may you begin to fully understand him. Hopefully, this compilation will provide a basis for that study.

James R. Fleming
Bolton, Tennessee
June 19, 1992

ACKNOWLEDGMENTS

I would like to acknowledge several organizations, contributors and well-wishers without whom this publication would not have been possible. First, I would like to thank Mr. Richard A. Shrader of the Southern Historical Collection, Library of the University of North Carolina at Chapel Hill for permission to use Captain James I. Hall's papers. Immense assistance was provided by Mr. Russell Bailey. Mr. David D. Barno has been invaluable and the maps were painstakingly researched and provided by Mr. Chuck Brown. I would also like to thank Dr. Martin Gordon of White Mane Publishing Co., Inc. for providing the final editing of this book.

Further assistance and inspiration was provided by Mr. James Allen Smith, Judge Mark A. Walker, Judge Wilbur Cash, Mr. Jim Phillips, Rev. John Gardner, Rev. Charles Todd, Mr. David Gwinn, Mrs. Donna Eason, Mrs. Rosella Hall, Ms. Sherl Rose, Ms. Sharon Short, Captain Mark Hubbs, Mr. Cheely Carter, Mr. Bob Parker, Mrs. Tirri Parker, Dr. Anthony Hodges, Mr. Michael Bub, Mr. & Mrs. Harry Bryan, the interpretative historians of the reenactment of Company C, 9th Tennessee Infantry, C.S.A.; Company B, 20th Tennessee Infantry, C.S.A.; Company D, 20th Kentucky Infantry, U.S.A.; Camp 257, Simonton/Wilcox Camp of the Sons of Confederate Veterans, and the Fort Wright Chapter of the United Daughters of the Confederacy, both of Covington, Tennessee.

Finally, I would like to thank my parents and my sister for their support and encouragement in this project: James McDill Fleming, Margie Elizabeth Fleming and Elizabeth Aileen Fleming.

INTRODUCTION

The men who formed Company C of the 9th Tennessee Infantry, known as the "Southern Confederates," came from the Mount Carmel, Covington, Mason, Stanton, Randolph, Mount Zion (Munford), and Portersville (Salem) communities of West Tennessee. Those communities were basically farming communities; however, this does not mean that they were uneducated nor poor. On the contrary, at least one third of the 126 men who left their homes and families that May morning were either college graduates or came directly from college to enlist. Of the other known professions, eleven were farmers, seven were laborers, five were teachers, four were clerks and two were ministers. This group also included at least one theological student, a carpenter, a merchant, a physician, and a silversmith.

Eight of the original members were married and three were widowers, two were without families and at least two others were married during the war. Their average age at the time of enlistment was twenty-two and a half. Fifty-five members were born in Tennessee, eleven in South Carolina, seven in Virginia, six in North Carolina, one in Alabama and four in Ireland.

The average height of the 9th Tennessee soldier, as taken from recorded Oaths of Allegiance and the Disability Certificates, was 5' 6", ranging from 5' to 6'4".

On the surface, Company C, the "Southern Confederates," or for that matter, the 9th Tennessee as a whole, was similar to other units of the Army of Tennessee. For example, the following chart compares Company C of the 9th Tennessee Infantry to Company H of the 1st Tennessee Infantry (Sam Watkins' company of "Co. Aytch" fame) and Company B of the 20th Tennessee Infantry:*

---

*Company H was in the same brigade from Shiloh to the end of the war. Company B was in a different brigade but in the same army.

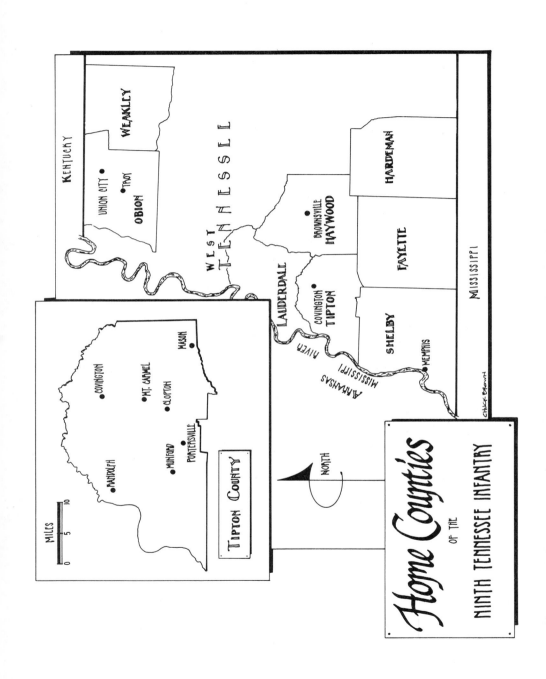

KENTUCKY

WEST TENNESSEE

WEAKLEY

UNION CITY
TROY
OBION

MISSISSIPPI

ARKANSAS

HARDEMAN

BROWNSVILLE
HAYWOOD

FAYETTE

LAUDERDALE

COVINGTON
TIPTON

SHELBY

MEMPHIS

MISSISSIPPI RIVER

CHUCK BROWN

MILES
0 5 10

COVINGTON
MT. CARMEL
CLOPTON
MASON
RANDOLPH
MUNFORD
PORTERSVILLE

TIPTON COUNTY

NORTH

Home Counties
OF THE
NINTH TENNESSEE INFANTRY

	1st Tenn. Co. H	9th Tenn. Co. C	20th Tenn. Co. B
Original Number in Co., 1861	120	126	159
Number of original soldiers remaining at Surrender, 1865	7	11	6
Original Number in Rgt., 1861	1250	Over 1000	900
Total Rgt. at Surrender, 1865	65	40	4

Twenty-seven of the "Southern Confederates'" original members were killed, fifty-five were wounded of which fifteen died, four were prisoners, fourteen deserted (many to join cavalry regiments) and eleven were present at the surrender.

Why did those men go to war? Though long in their graves, we have here the rare opportunity to let the soldiers answer for themselves. In Captain Wood's reply to Miss Thompson at the presentation of Company C's flag at Clopton's Campground (see page 17), he stated: "The rights, equality and justice for which our fathers fought have been denied us, our overtures for peace and justice have been treated with contempt; our arguments and entreaties have been met with insults, and we are now menaced with invasion. There is no alternative left us but to meet the fanatic on the battlefield."

But the predominant question is: After so many hardships and so many losses, why did they keep on fighting even when failure seemed inevitable? Though those men were fighting for their homes and their way of life, after years of hard campaigning, the shining glow of patriotism faded from their faces and primal instincts engulfed them. During the shock of battle, high ideals left their minds and they fought simply for survival. They fought with and for their brothers—both their brothers by blood and their brothers by fire. As many as 26 sets of brothers entered military service under the "Southern Confederates'" banner. By April of 1865, all were brothers.

Individually, the "Southern Confederates" were one of the most well educated, zealously religious and unbelievably gallant group of men with a devotion to duty unequaled in either army—an immortal Band of Brothers.

THE STORY OF COMPANY C, 9TH TENNESSEE INFANTRY

"Southern Confederates"
Company C
9th Tennessee Infantry

On April 23, 1861, Tipton County, Tennessee citizens met at the Mountain Academy to organize a company of volunteer soldiers in response to the Confederates' firing on Fort Sumter. Seventeen men enrolled at that time. Two days later, their ranks swelled to sixty as they met at Clopton's Campground and officially named their company "The Southern Confederates." They elected their officers as they began camp life: David Josiah Wood, captain; James Iredell Hall, first lieutenant; Charles Bryson Simonton, second lieutenant; and Robert W. Lemmon, third lieutenant.

Uniform material consisting of a rough, dingy, slaty colored gray jeans was procured. Collars and seams of the pants were adorned with a calico of sickly hospital yellow, and their shirts were of a hickory (checkered) color. None of their uniforms survived the war but their coats might have been made in a tunic or frock style.

Approximately one month after its organization, the "Southern Confederates" prepared to move to Camp Beauregard in Jackson, Tennessee for enlistment into the Confederate ranks. But before their departure, a beautiful First National pattern Confederate flag was presented to them by the ladies of Tipton County. It is said that it was the regimental banner used both at the battles of Shiloh and Perryville.

On May 22, 1861, the "Southern Confederates" were mustered into Confederate service as Company C of the 9th Tennessee Infantry and immediately went into a camp of instruction at Union City, Tennessee and remained there for two months. There the 6th and 9th Tennessee Infantry Regiments were first brigaded together in Brigadier General Benjamin F. Cheatham's Brigade, in which they remained for the balance of the war. Prior to this time, large knives made by a local blacksmith was their only weapon. But in Union City, antiquated flintlock muskets were issued to Company C.

Beginning August 1, 1861, Company C marched from Union City, Tennessee to New Madrid, Missouri and then to Columbus, Kentucky. There they were held in reserve during the Battle of Belmont and afterwards were moved back to Columbus and remained there throughout the winter.

On March 1, 1862, the army began a march to Union City, then by railroad to Corinth, Mississippi. On April 4, the 9th Tennessee Infantry marched sixteen miles through mud and water and camped on the battlefield of Shiloh. Under the orders of Cheatham, the regiment was held in reserve until 10 o'clock, at which time they were thrown into the thickest of the battle, later called "The Hornet's Nest." They were later shifted to another portion of the field and at 2 o'clock were ordered to charge across a peach orchard. During the night, a train of artillery (thought to be Morton's battery) separated the 9th Tennessee Infantry and neither knew the whereabouts of the other. Captain D. J. Wood of Company C was assigned to one section. They fought in front of Shiloh Church throughout the next day. Here occurred some of the hardest fighting of the war. Nineteen men were killed and seventy were wounded. In the two days, the regiment lost 60 men. They retreated until 9 o'clock and reached Corinth, Mississippi the next day where they remained for seven weeks.

On May 8, 1862, the regiment was reorganized and Charles Bryson Simonton was elected captain. During this period, Ordnance Sergeant James Spense requisitioned 11,000 Buck and Ball cartridges and 12,000 percussion caps. This leads us to believe that .69 caliber smoothbore percussion muskets (the most common, being the model 1842 or the converted model 1822) were in use at that time.

Conditions at Corinth became unhealthy which necessitated a move to Tupelo, Mississippi. It was here that Buford ordered 31 enameled haversacks (probably similar to the Union tarred haversacks).

From Tupelo, the army was transferred by railroad to Mobile, Alabama, then to Chattanooga by way of Montgomery, Alabama and Atlanta, Georgia. From here, the Kentucky Campaign began. They marched across the Cumberland Mountains northward to

Tompkinsville, then Glasgow, Kentucky. They were in Glasgow when the Battle of Munfordsville occurred some twenty miles away.

The next morning, a sixty-mile march to Bardstown began, from there, Lebanon, Perryville, Danville and then Harrodsburg. After a stay of two or three days, they marched back to Perryville and were formed into a line of battle. The morning was spent shifting their position to and fro until about three o'clock in the afternoon. The 9th Tennessee Infantry was in a line of battle directly across the field from a six gun battery of Napoleons (12 pounder smoothbore bronze cannons) commanded by Captain Charles Parsons and Brigadier General William R. Terrill's infantry. Dividing them was a worm fence that delayed their assault and resulted in many casualties. Cheatham's replacement, Brigadier General George Maney, ordered the charge, and young Robert H. Gibbs placed the banner of Company C upon the central gun of the battery just prior to his death. The guns were captured and were used by the brigade until they were lost at the Battle of Nashville.

Maney's Brigade (of which the 9th Tennessee was a part) forced the Federals off the field for a distance of two miles but at a great price. Of the regiment, 52 men were killed and 76 wounded—most of which fell into the hands of the enemy as General Braxton Bragg ordered a withdrawal. This constituted a loss of nearly one-fourth the number of the regiment.

After the battle, the Confederate troops made a rapid march to Knoxville, Tennessee and then on to Murfreesboro. At that time, the 6th and 9th Tennessee Infantries were officially consolidated, but they still kept separate rosters.

On the morning of December 31, 1862, the 9th Tennessee crossed Stones River and took position in an open field, but was initially held in reserve. Much confusion existed as to the identity of the ranks to their front on the Wilkerson turnpike. Their identity remained a mystery until many of General George Maney's Brigade were dead. General B. F. Cheatham led the charge which pushed the Federal line into a cedar thicket and over a hill beyond for five miles. This position was held throughout the night. It was intensely cold, but fires could not be built for fear of snipers. After Major General John C. Breckinridge's unsuccessful charge the next day failed, the Confederate army retired to Shelbyville, Tennessee and went into winter quarters until the last of June when, by slow marches, they fell back to Chattanooga and remained there until the middle of September.

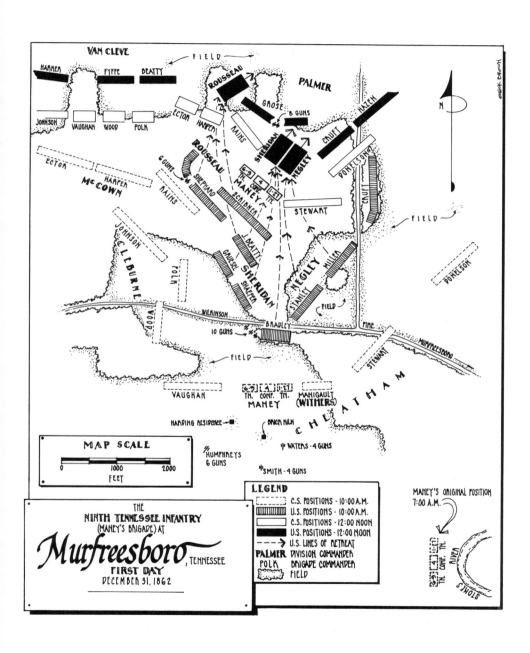

VAN CLEVE

FIELD

HARKER FYFFE BEATTY ROUSSEAU PALMER

JOHNSON VAUGHAN WOOD POLK ECTOR HARPER GROSE 8 GUNS HAZEN

NAINS SHERIDAN CRUFT

ECTOR HARPER ROUSSEAU DONELSON

McCOWN 6 GUNS SHEPARD SCRIBNER TN-9 CONF. TN NEGLEY CRUFT

NAINS MANEY STEWART FIELD

JOHNSON J. BEATTY NEGLEY MILLER

CLEBURNE POLK GRUSEL SHERIDAN STANLEY MILLER DONELSON

WOOD SHAFER FIELD

WILKINSON PIKE

10 GUNS BRADLEY MURFREESBORO

FIELD STEWART

CHEATHAM

VAUGHAN TN-9 CONF. TN MANIGAULT (WITHERS)

MANEY

HARDING RESIDENCE BRICK KILN

WATERS - 4 GUNS

HUMPHREYS 6 GUNS

SMITH - 4 GUNS

MAP SCALE

0   1000   2000

FEET

THE
NINTH TENNESSEE INFANTRY
(MANEY'S BRIGADE) AT

Murfreesboro, TENNESSEE

FIRST DAY
DECEMBER 31, 1862

LEGEND

☐ C.S. POSITIONS - 10:00 A.M.
▨ U.S. POSITIONS - 10:00 A.M.
☐ C.S. POSITIONS - 12:00 NOON
■ U.S. POSITIONS - 12:00 NOON
▬ ▬ ▬ U.S. LINES OF RETREAT
PALMER DIVISION COMMANDER
POLK BRIGADE COMMANDER
FIELD

MANEY'S ORIGINAL POSITION
7:00 A.M.

TN-9 CONF. TN

RIVER

STONES

Private John Cavanaugh of Company H stated, at that time: "We were reduced in rations to three cast iron crackers and five ounces of bacon a day. Bragg's Commissary General seemed to think that members of the rank and file could march and fight on ten ounces of food a day."

The morning of Saturday, September 19, 1863, the 9th Tennessee Infantry was thrown into a line of battle shortly after crossing Chickamauga Creek for the Battle of Chickamauga. They had to march at the right oblique over ground covered with felled timber and piles of wood which forced gaps in their line. After passing about 80 yards over a slight elevation, Colonel Joseph B. Dodge's Brigade of Brigadier General Richard W. Johnson's Division opened a concentrated fire, there being no one to the regiment's left. The Federals were almost completely out of sight of the 9th. By then, the 9th's ammunition was low and the Federals had advanced at a rapid pace. This forced the Confederates to retire or they would certainly be killed or captured. During this engagement, two-thirds of the regiment were lost. Twenty-five men were killed and 155 were wounded, 17 of whom later died. Sunday, September 20, 1863, the regiment was once again brought into a line of battle at about 2 P.M. Saturday, they fought on the extreme left of the army and Sunday, on the extreme right. The enemy was outflanked and pressed to such a degree that a full rout resulted. Breckinridge's Division passed over the breastworks to the regiment's left shortly before dark as the 9th Tennessee bivouacked for the night inside the enemy's breastworks.

After the battle of Chickamauga, the enemy was pursued until they reached Missionary Ridge. They fortified the ridge but Confederate forces, including the 9th Tennessee, charged bayonets and forced the Federals to flee pell-mell down the other side thus bottling them up in Chattanooga until the last week of November.

The 9th was stationed on Lookout Mountain on November 23, 1863. The next day, they were marched to Missionary Ridge which left Lookout Mountain, as one participant stated, "almost without defenders." That was the day the "Battle above the Clouds" was fought. But, according to Hall and others there, it was just a skirmish. Two days later, the Federal army advanced up Missionary Ridge. The 9th was held in reserve supporting the 1st and 27th Tennessee Infantry regiments of their brigade, who were opposing 6 brigades and 3 regiments from Major General O. O. Howard's Corps, but a few men of the company were ordered into action against Federal sharpshooters. Unable to return their fire without exposing themselves, they rolled boulders down the ridge, dislodging the Yankees from their positions. About nine o'clock that night, as Company C was cooking supper and bedding down for the night, they were ordered to abandon their position and retreat south as part of the rear guard.

The night march that ensued was bitterly cold. The rear guard was cut off from the rest of the army and a detour across Chickamauga Creek was forced. Just prior to this crossing, a small battle called Cat Creek ensued in which Maney was wounded. Sometime after dark, they reached Dalton, Georgia where they remained in winter quarters for four months.

Much change occurred during these four months. General Braxton Bragg was replaced with General Joseph E. Johnston, to the adulation of the Army of Tennessee. In an effort to unite his command he immediately increased rations to his troops and also ordered a new battle flag to be issued that was based on the Virginia battle flag.

On May 7, 1864, as Major General William T. Sherman advanced on Dalton, the Army of Tennessee was placed on Rocky Face Ridge on either side of a gap that led into the town which forced the Federals to flank the Confederates, precipitating a retreat to Resaca. The 9th Tennessee once again performed rear guard duties as entrenchments were already dug by the time they arrived prior to the engagement. Approximately May 15, they were placed in position behind a battery and were bombarded for two days but could not return their fire. Basically this was a drawn battle. The Union lost 4,000 and the Confederates 3,000 effectives.

On May 17, 1864, the 9th Tennessee was involved in a sharp engagement at Adairsville, Georgia. Being posted in front of Turner's Mississippi battery, they faced the enemy across an open field. Eight days later, they participated in a battle that was fought in a thunderstorm at New Hope Church. Two days after that, Company C participated in the battle of Dallas, Georgia. It was here that General John C. Breckinridge led his troops in a frontal assault across an open field.

June 27, 1864, found Maney's Brigade squarely in the thickest of the fight with Sherman's forces at Kennessaw Mountain. Positioned in an extremely vulnerable precipitous position dubbed the "Dead Angle," with others of the brigade, the 9th Tennessee withstood the brunt of an entire corps aligned in five lines of battle. Lasting approximately one hour, firing became so incessant that in at least one instance, lead bullets were melting as they were loaded into the barrels of their guns. At one point, the 6th and 9th Tennessee were called to assist the 1st and 27th Tennessee by moving up the very steep hill (now known as Cheatham's Hill) to their position while still firing. The Federals eventually flanked the Confederate army, once more forcing another evacuation.

Prior to the next engagement, the Confederate Army of Tennessee was dealt a blow far worse than Sherman's Army of the Tennessee could have inflicted. This was the replacement of General Joseph E. Johnston as their commander by General John B. Hood. Men who never even suggested the idea thought seriously of desertion. On July 20, 1864, Hood ordered his first attack at a place called Peach Tree Creek. Maney's Division, of which the 9th Tennessee was a member, was the only full division engaged here. They were thrown into three fully entrenched lines of the enemy. They drove the enemy from the first two lines but were halted before they could dislodge them from the third. The Confederates held the field as the enemy withdrew. Two days later, the bloody and disastrous Battle of Decatur, also known as the Battle of Atlanta, occurred. Cheatham and Cleburne's men attacked General James M. McPherson's men in a hand to hand struggle. Maney's Brigade was said to have been the first that passed the enemy works and to have pressed farther forward than any portion of the Confederate line. Of the 9th Tennessee, one fifth of the number engaged were casualties.

After the fall of Atlanta, the army slowly fell back to Jonesboro. The 9th was not heavily engaged here but the rest of Cheatham and Cleburne's men held the line in check for hours against overwhelming odds. General George W. Gordon's Brigade was the principal participant in this engagement. In the short time he was in command, Hood had lost over one-third of the army either killed or wounded.

On August 31, 1864, two of Maney's brigades attacked entrenched Federals under General O. O. Howard at Jonesboro, Georgia. The charge was repulsed at great loss to the Confederates. Maney resigned after this battle.

During the engagements at Spring Hill and Franklin, the 9th Tennessee Infantry's Brigade was commanded by Brigadier General John C. Carter—the division, by Major General John C. Brown.

Shortly after the battle of Jonesboro, a sharp engagement occurred at Lovejoy Station in which the 9th Tennessee was involved. After this battle, Hood's army turned north. There were light engagements at Dalton, Georgia and at Decatur and Florence, Alabama.

At Spring Hill, Tennessee, Brown's attack was to be the signal for the other brigades to attack but for fear of being outflanked, he refused to engage the enemy. The Army of Tennessee then camped for the night near Columbia Pike between Major General John M. Schofield's Army of the Ohio and Franklin, Tennessee. But during the night, Schofield quietly marched his entire army past the Confederates into the town of Franklin and began fortifying it.

On November 30, 1864, General John B. Hood marched his army across two miles of open fields into entrenched Union troops. Their breastworks were prepared two years earlier by Confederates and fortified the day previous. The 9th Tennessee passed through a locust thicket into a galling fire. Cheatham's old division alone held its ground. They were on one side of the breastworks and the Federals on the other. Fighting continued into the night when the Federals withdrew to Nashville. The men of Company C never knew whom they were fighting.

November 30th was an Indian summer day. Shortly afterwards, rain, sleet and snow began to fall, making a bad situation even worse. What was left of Hood's Army of Tennessee laid siege to Nashville for two weeks and on December 15, 1864, Union Major General George H. Thomas attacked. Cheatham's Division was on the right of the army on the first day's battle and moved to the army's left for the second day's battle. On this day, the 9th Tennessee was exposed to great peril, having the enemy on both flanks before defeat was realized. They were drawn up for battle on the back side of one of the Overton Hills (now called Shy's Hill). Federal cavalry under Colonel Datus E. Coon flanked Lieutenant Colonel Zachariah L. Watters' (formerly Gist's), Maney's (formerly John C. Carter's) and Govan's Brigades, using Spencer repeating carbines to force their retreat. On the retreat through Franklin, Private John Pruitt (a member of Company H, 9th Tennessee, who was on cooking detail) handed each member of the company a piece of half-baked bread which was soft from the rain. It was the only ration they had had for twenty-four hours previous and would have for thirty-six hours afterwards. According to Private John Cavanaugh, also of Company H: "We were in a woe-begone plight. A thin jacket, thin cotton pants, most of us barefoot; we looked as if, put in a field, we would have been taken for scarecrows."

Federal cavalry once again attacked the 6th and 9th Tennessee in the retreat but soon realized that they had run up against, as one participant put it, "The business end of a hornet." Once again, the Tennesseans had to repulse the enemy near Spring Hill. The retreat was pressed fiercely and engaged about every hour from Columbia to Pulaski. Between Lynnville and Richland Creek, the fighting was incessant. At the Elk River, the Federal advance received a brutal repulse. The Confederates eventually re-crossed

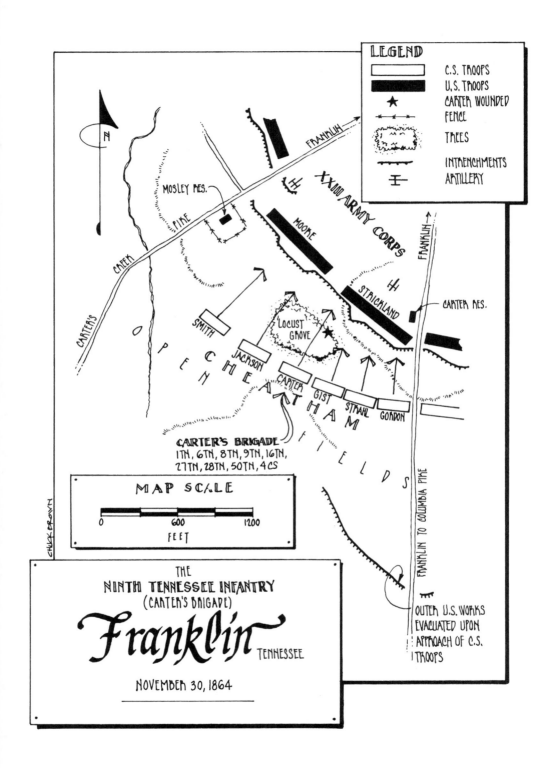

LEGEND

C.S. TROOPS
U.S. TROOPS
CARTER WOUNDED
FENCE
TREES
INTRENCHMENTS
ARTILLERY

FRANKLIN

N

MOSLEY RES.

PIKE

CREEK

CARTERS

XXIII ARMY CORPS

MOORE

STRICKLAND

FRANKLIN

CARTER RES.

SMITH

LOCUST GROVE

JACKSON

O P E N   C H E A T H A M   F I E L D S

CARTER

GIST

STRAHL

GORDON

CARTER'S BRIGADE
1TH, 6TH, 8TH, 9TH, 16TH,
27TH, 28TH, 50TH, 4 CS

MAP SCALE

0   600   1200
FEET

CHUCK BROWN

FRANKLIN TO COLUMBIA PIKE

OUTER U.S. WORKS
EVACUATED UPON
APPROACH OF C.S.
TROOPS

THE
NINTH TENNESSEE INFANTRY
(CARTER'S BRIGADE)
Franklin TENNESSEE

NOVEMBER 30, 1864

the Tennessee River and moved on to Corinth, Mississippi. At this time, the 6th and the 9th were furloughed until February 10, 1865.

Most of the Army of Tennessee left Tupelo, Mississippi in late January for North Carolina. The entire army was supposed to meet at West Point, Mississippi but when the 6th and the 9th arrived, they discovered that the rest of the army had left two weeks earlier. Many of these men joined Major General Nathan Bedford Forrest's Cavalry and eventually surrendered with him in Alabama. However, the remaining eleven veterans of Company C, 9th Tennessee, traveled from Tupelo on foot to West Point, Mississippi and arrived there on January 28. They rode the railroad through Meridian and Demopolis to Selma, Alabama. There they went by steamship to Montgomery and from there by train to Columbus, Georgia. From Columbus, they marched through Macon and Milledgeville to Mayfield where they once again rode the railroad to Augusta. From Augusta, they marched to Newbery, South Carolina and joined General Stevenson's Corps. The next day, they participated in skirmishes in such a manner as General Joseph E. Johnston commented to General P. G. T. Beauregard of the bravery and dash of Stewart and Cheatham's men.

March 19, 1865, brought on the final battle for the Army of Tennessee at Bentonville, but Cheatham's men were delayed in the rail yards at Salisbury. The Federals pressed the Confederate army on April 6 and moved on Smithfield on the 10th. Johnston retreated through Raleigh, Chapel Hill, Salem and then to Greensboro, North Carolina—burning bridges behind him.

On April 14, Johnston sent a courier into the Union lines with a request for a truce while terms for surrender were discussed. Finally, on April 26, 1865, the arms of Company C, 9th Tennessee Infantry were stacked around a tall tree and their battle flag was torn into fragments and distributed among its members as they bravely accepted their fate.

The long trek home took the Tipton Countians through the Blue Ridge Mountains to Ashville, North Carolina, down the French Broad River to Paint Rock and across the mountains to Greenville, Tennessee. There they were met by U.S. Colored Troops who confiscated their horses and side arms, crowded them into box cars and sent them to Knoxville. From there they were sent to Chattanooga then Nashville. Then they were put on a steamer and sent down the Cumberland River to the Ohio River on to the Mississippi River, down to Fort Pillow and finally, home.

CHAPTER 1

COMPANY C, 9TH TENNESSEE

Reunion of the Surviving Members at Capt. James I. Hall's
A Day of Genuine Delight for the Veterans.

The reunion of Company C, Ninth Tennessee regiment seems to have been a very much enjoyed affair. Those who participated in it were highly delighted, enthusiastic in fact.

The attendance was strictly limited to survivors of the company and their families and the families of deceased comrades.

Company C, the famous "Southern Confederates," claims to have been the first company organized in Tipton county: It was uniformed and equipped by private enterprise and tendered its services quite a while before the State seceded; the material of which it was composed constituted the flower of the old South; twenty-three of its members were graduates of college or came from college to the company. First and last it numbered about 126 men. Of this number 32 yet survive; 30 were killed in battle, 12 fell victims to the ravages of diseases of the camp, 26 were wounded and disabled. Only 11 were in line on the day of the surrender in North Carolina. Of the survivors ten gathered on the beautiful lawn of Capt. James I. Hall on the 24th, namely Capts. D.J. Wood, James I. Hall and C.B. Simonton, Messrs. J.W. Lemmon, J.S. Hill, J. Forsyth, F. Payne, D.M. McLennan, N. Kimbrough and S.E. Sweet. Their wives and children, together with those of some deceased comrades, made up a party of about forty-eight persons present who reported for duty.

The day was ideal—not a cloud and neither hot nor chilly: The spot selected the prettiest in all the county. The affair was alto-

1

gether informal: no program and nobody wanted to show off, everybody at home. It is true there had been a meeting of the company beforehand to prepare for the reunion and Capt. James I. Hall was chairman and this organization was still in existence, but its hand was not visible; everyone did what seemed right in his own eyes and all seemed to do exactly the right thing.

A little past eleven o'clock Capt. Simonton was requested to call the roll of the company. This seemed as if it would be short work and a very perfunctory duty, but it proved to be a highly interesting exercise. As each name was called, if the person was absent, some statement was made of his whereabouts, surroundings and prospects in life. The survivors were found to be scattered from Kentucky to Texas and from Tennessee to Arkansas and California. Interesting letters and postal cards were also read from absent comrades in reply to invitations sent them, regretting their inability to be present and expressing tender regard for the survivors and the memory of the dead. When the name of a dead comrade was read, a statement was made of when and where he died or was killed, with some of the facts connected therewith, or some illustration of his character, and if any family survived him something was given of their whereabouts and conditions in life. When the reader of the roll was in doubt he called upon the comrades present for their information, and often-times they volunteered mighty interesting information regarding both dead and living comrades.

This exercise occupied about one hour and a quarter and during this time every member of Company C was remembered and nearly every one of them passed in loving review before the survivors present and their interested families.

Then came dinner. You have seen and enjoyed tempting, appetizing, exquisite, bountiful and prodigal dinners, but from all accounts none to surpass this one, perhaps none to equal it.

After dinner comrade S.E. Sweet, of Forrest City, Ark., who lost the whole of his right arm at Chickamauga, besides receiving a painful and dangerous wound in the face and head, and who in camp and on the march beguiled more weary hours and turned them into pleasure than any other man in the army, an irrepressible, fun-loving and mirth-provoking fellow, who has never tired, always cheerful, and in the hour of danger as resolute, aggressive and cool as an ideal soldier—after dinner Mr. Sweet was introduced to tell some reminiscences. He was too modest to stand, but sitting entertained the whole company of persons present for something like three quarters of an hour with side-splitting and sometime pathetic stories, told in his original manner. Emory, as everybody calls him, could give Private John Allen and our Bob pointers on telling a war story.

At a business meeting of the company it was resolved to have a reunion next year, to be held at the same place on Thursday, the 25th of September.

An historical committee, consisting of Capt. James I. Hall, C.B. Simonton and Joe Forsyth, were appointed to gather and preserve facts connected with the history of the company and its members, and a resolution was also passed requesting each survivor and friend of the company to write down the facts within his knowledge and send to the historical committee.

Altogether it was, from the testimony of those participating, as enjoyable a reunion as has ever been held: everyone present expressed a desire to attend another.

Photographer Crunk was on hand and caught the shadows of the old soldiers and their families also. We understand the pictures are excellent.

Reunion of Company C, 9th Tennessee Infantry
Taken on the lawn of Captain Hall's home by Frank D. Crunk of Covington on Sept. 24, 1896. (L to R) Captains David Josiah Wood, Charles Bryson Simonton and James Iredell Hall, Privates Daniel M. McLennan, S. Emory Sweet, James W. Lemmon, Nat Kimbrough, Jonathan Sloan Hill, Romulus Payne and Joseph H. Forsythe.

A Letter From Mr. Emory Sweet About the Reunion.

Editors Leader — You will please allow me space in your columns to thank the members of Company C, their wives and children for the courtesies extended my wife, daughter and self at the reunion on the 24th. No manlier, braver set of men ever lived or died than Tipton county's first company that was organized at the old Clopton Campground, officered by D.J. Wood, James I. Hall, C.B. Simonton and Robert Lemmon.

I wish you could have seen the ten battle-scarred veterans and their families on the 24th and especially when Joe Forsyth announced dinner. Sloan and Jim were always regarded by the boys as GOOD FIGHTERS and eaters as Company C had, but we now consider them the BEST EATERS and not such good fighters.

Capts. Hall, Simonton and Jim Lemmon have always occupied a warm place in my heart, but their generous hospitality at the reunion has placed me under lasting obligations to them, their noble wives, accomplished daughters and worthy sons will ever by remembered by Mrs. Sweet and my daughter as an oasis in the desert of life that eternity can not eradicate.

Well do I remember as if but yesterday thirty-five years ago last May at old Clopton, when we bade adieu to mothers, fathers, sisters, brothers wives and sweethearts, amid tears and prayers, for Jackson, Tenn. We felt then we could whip "16 to 1," but ere a few weeks death furloughed Dan Calhoun. Dan was the pride of Company C. We will never forget Dan's death; he was the first member of Company C who sickened and died. More anon.

Forrest City, Ark., Sept. 28, 1896 Emory Sweet.

Souvenir Walking Stick

Made from the tree around which Sergeant N.S. Carrothers of Co. E, 9th Tennessee Infantry stacked his rifle at the surrender. Carved (oral history states that it was burned with a hot wire) in the stick is: N.S. Carrothers, 9th Tenn Regt, May 1865, also the battles of Shiloh, Perryville, Murfreesboro, Chickamauga, Mission Ridge, Cat Creek, Resaca, Adairsville, Rockyface, New Hope, Kennesaw Mt., Dallas, Peachtree Creek, Atlanta, Jonesboro, Lovejoy, Dalton, Franklin, Overton Hill and Nashville. Also, Sgt. Carrothers' fellow parolees carved their initials in the walking stick. They are the initials of: Pvt. J.H. Layton of Co. E, 1st Sgt. R.W. Davis of Co. G, Pvt. J.M. Bell of Co. H, 1st Lt. R.J. Dew of Co. G, Pvt. William Henry Hiliard of Co. G, Pvt. G.W. Carmack of Co. H, Corp.

T.J. Latimer of Co. H and the unidentified initials of A.N.Y. Owned by Sgt. Carrothers great grandson, Dr. Snowden C. Carruthers, the walking stick was broken when Sgt. Carrothers threw it at a hog sometime after the war.

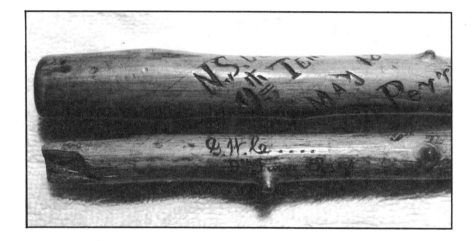

CHAPTER 2

CHARLES BRYSON SIMONTON
1838–1911

A prominent citizen of what is now the Salem Community, Charles Bryson Simonton, served the people of Portersville and later Tipton County, Tennessee. Portersville was established by James Hodges in 1831 and continued as the center of the community until after the coming of the railroad in 1872.

Captain
Charles Bryson Simonton
1838–1911

Charles B. Simonton was born in Tipton County in 1838 and was a graduate of Erskine College in Due West, South Carolina graduating in 1859.

There was a school in the south end of the village of Portersville, which was destroyed by fire in 1863. Simonton taught school there after his graduation from college in 1859.

Simonton enlisted as a private in Company C, 9th Tennessee Infantry, and subsequently rose to the rank of captain. Severely wounded in the arm at the Battle of Perryville, Kentucky in 1862, he was disabled from any further active duty during the war. At this time, Captain Simonton, at the solicitation of old friends, took charge of the school in the fall of 1863.

There being no school building in Portersville after the fire nor any nearby except the privately owned Wilson schoolhouse near the Salem Associate Reformed Presbyterian Church, Simonton opened a school in the church through the courtesy of its officials. He continued teaching there for several years as a majority of the patrons of the Portersville Academy were members of the church. During the first years after the war, Professor H. M. Lynn, a classmate of Captain Simonton, was associated with him at the Academy. He remained at the school for some time after the captain entered the realm of politics.

This school was an incorporated institution, controlled by a board of trustees, and was enjoying greater rights and privileges than were ordinarily conferred on "old field schools." The Academy always employed college trained men as principals, which was rarely the case in schools in the county.

Captain Simonton remained at the head of the school until 1868 when he was elected circuit court clerk. In 1870, he was, again, elected clerk of the circuit court of Tipton County, and he took advantage of the opportunity to study law.

Simonton began his practice in Covington in 1873 after being admitted to the bar. Four years later, he was elected to the Tennessee legislature and became editor of the *Tipton Record*—a paper later to be absorbed by *The Covington Leader*. He was elected to the Forty-Sixth Congress in 1879 and was re-elected for a second term two years later. He served as chairman of the Tennessee Democratic Convention in 1886. Six years later, he was a presidential elector on the Democratic ticket of President Grover Cleveland.

In his latter years, Simonton served as president of the Covington city school board and was a United States district attorney for the district of Tennessee from 1895 until 1898.

He died in Covington in 1911 and is buried in the Munford Cemetery.

(Historical Research by James Allen Smith, January 24, 1972.)

A Soldier's Recollections

*Brief Sketch of the Organization of
Company C, 9th Tennessee Regiment.*

Editors Leader—At your request and that of several other friends, I now furnish you some of the principal facts in regard to Company C. Ninth Tennessee Regiment, recited by me in my remarks at the

Captain Charles Bryson Simonton
(in later years)
1838–1911

unveiling of the monument on the 29th of May, 1895, together with
some introductory statements, and so give those who feel inclined
an opportunity to file away this much of the record of this gallant
company.

Captains D.J. Wood and James I. Hall were the principal movers
and promoters in enlisting and organizing the company. They took
steps in this direction a few days after Ft. Sumter was fired on, by
calling a meeting at the Mountain Academy, where Capt. Hall was

teaching school, as he now is and has been since the close of the war. I had just closed my second session of school at the Portersville Academy with the parade of a public examination and an exhibition at night. The Mountain, Portersville and even Covington were rural districts then, without railroad connection, and the news of public affairs traveled slowly. At Portersville we had a mail only twice a week by horseback rider from Covington to Raleigh. The evening my school closed the Memphis Appeal was received, which gave account of the firing upon Ft. Sumter, but with my duties as master of a school and manager of what I thought was a great exhibition, I never saw the paper or knew of the actual opening of the civil war until the next morning.

Within two or three days I received by messenger a note requesting my presence at the meeting called to be held at the Mountain Academy.

Up to this time Tennessee had declined to secede. Isham G. Harris was governor of the State and known to be in favor of secession, but he had no power to call for volunteers and no way to maintain, or arm and equip them if their services should be tendered him, but we were well satisfied that if we organized ourselves into a company he would never order us to disperse. The old men of the Mountain, Dickey Hall, Lansing Hall, John N. Hall, James W. Hall, Mr. Stitt, Mr. Elam, the Calhouns—in fact, all the old men in the community—were there.

There were no fiery speeches; they were all of one mind. Lincoln had called for the 75,000 ninety-day volunteers; the war, they thought, was inevitable. How to arm, equip and maintain a company until the state might secede, or if she failed to do so, then until our services might be accepted by the Confederacy, were the questions discussed. Calculations were made and it was determined that at least $5000 would be necessary, and within a few hundred of this amount was subscribed within a few minutes. The enlistments as I remember were 25 or 26. It was determined to hold another meeting a few days later at Clopton Campground to secure the remaining subscriptions necessary and procure further enlistments. A paper was given me to secure enlistments at and around Portersville. I also gave one for a like purpose to my friend and former classmate, H.M. Lynn, who was teaching school at Mount Zion. A paper for enlistments was also sent to Covington, but I do not remember to whom. As I recall it, Jas. W. Hall presided over the meeting at the Mountain and Benjamin Adams over the meeting at Clopton. At this latter meeting the subscription was completed and a number of additional recruits had been obtained, though the directions were not to solicit any recruits except persons of good

character and steady habits. A day was set for the election of officers and organization of the company. I am sorry I have no memo-
randa to give me the exact date, but I am sure it was not later than
the first of May 1861, and I think it was about the 25th of April. We
met in the old Clopton church, across the branch from its present
location. Capt. Wood, a man of sturdy virtues and who had had
some experience in a campaign to Mexico, was elected captain by
acclamation. We looked up to him as the fountain of all military
knowledge. Capt. Hall, with a like unanimity, was made first lieutenant. He attempted, with great sincerity, to decline the honor,
preferring to carry a musket and march in the ranks. He gave it as
his honest opinion that he was poorly adapted to perform the duties of an officer, but he thought he could carry a gun well enough
and make a pretty fair private soldier. The boys admired him for his
modesty, but passed on to second Lieutenant. Some gentleman
proposed my name. Taking the cue from Lieut. Hall, I protested. It
is very probable I was also very sincere, for I did not know the
simplest military maneuvers or word of command even and I guess
it occurred to me just then that an officer was expected to lead the
men always in the face of danger, and if need be, to teach them by
example how to die, and these reflections made me modest. I really
wanted to avoid that post of distinction and—danger. Robt. W.
Lemmon, a delicate and gentle-mannered, boyish-looking young
man, but, as the sequel showed, of very cool courage, was chosen
without opposition as third Lieutenant. At the expiration of our
term of enlistment, twelve months, the company was reorganized
instead of disbanding, and in the reorganization Lieut. Lemmon
declined to stand for reelection and took his place as a private in
the company, where he had served as an officer. He was subsequently discharged on account of feeble health, but declined to be
released from duty, and fell while fighting in the ranks at New Hope
Church in the Georgia campaign, 1864, with his discharge in his
pocket. Peace to his memory.

There was a spirited contest over the election of non-commis-
sioned officers, except as to orderly sergeant. To this place J.D.
Calhoun, whom all the boys called Dan, was elected by acclamation. He was a brother-in-law of Capt. D.J. Wood, a popular young
man, recently married; and his memory is invested with special
interest because he was the first victim in our company to the casualties of war. He sickened and died while we were in the camp of
instruction at Union City—almost before we were accustomed to
camp duties. When the election was over the roll of officers stood
as follows:

Commissioned officers, D.J. Wood Captain, Jas. I. Hall first lieutenant, C.B. Simonton second lieutenant, Robert W. Lemmon third lieutenant; sergeant, J.D. Calhoun orderly sergeant, W.H. Foster, second sergeant, J.R. McCreight third sergeant, S.J. Bradshaw fourth sergeant; corporals, M. Munford first corporal, H.M. Lynn second corporal, Wm. Camp Bell third corporal, Newt McMullen fourth corporal.

The above men were the offices we were entitled to fill, but having our hand in, we proceeded to elect a commissary, an ensign, a surgeon and a chaplain, so that to the roster above given there was this addition: Wm. Young ensign, Ed Jones commissary, T.A. Kyle surgeon, J.W. Winford chaplain.

The company consisted rank and file of sixty men, but applications for enlistment were constantly coming in. It was solemnly resolved that no more recruits would be received except by the vote of the whole company and all applications were thereafter voted on with the particularity of a secret order in receiving new members. We then adopted as our company's name that of "Southern Confederates." We were ordered by our gallant captain into camp immediately. We found the tents and other conveniences of the camp ground well adapted to breaking us gradually into camp life. Each volunteer brought his blanket; our home people supplied us with choice rations, the young ladies cheered us almost daily with their presence. It was a sort of picnic time, but we managed to get a "Hardees' Tactics" and learned something about forming line, counting off by twos and fours, right face, front, right dress, and we marched around to the monotone hep, hep of our gallant captain, and at the word hep we brought down our left foot with a tremendous stamp that almost made the earth tremble.

At our organization, a committee was appointed to purchase uniforms for the whole company, which soon reached the full limit of 100 men rank and file, and to procure blankets etc., for these who were unable to provide for themselves conveniently. Gray was already the color of the Confederacy, but gray cloth was scarce. Our committee had difficulty in procuring enough cloth of any kind to make 106 uniform suits. The merchants of Memphis offered to have some beautiful jeans ordered from the factories in North Carolina, but the demand was so great that it would probably be several weeks before orders could be filled, and we really feared we would be in the midst of active service and perhaps the war ended before we could get our uniforms. Finally several hundred yards of a dingy, slaty colored jeans (it was mere courtesy to call it gray, and it was rough finished at that) was found and selected by the committee.[1] To say the boys who were expecting an elegant uniform were disappointed is putting it mildly; but they came nearer rebelling still when they saw the calico of a sickly hospital yellow which was to make the stripes on the pants and adorn the collars of the coats. Each volunteer considered himself a gentleman as well as a soldier, but when the tailors came to take our measure and the good women and patriotic ladies with their offer to make up the garments, all was serene once more. So it was that various associations tended not only to make our uniforms bearable, but when we finally donned them with our hickory shirts, we were really proud of them, as well as ourselves, and we just wished the whole Yankee nation could see us once in the performance of such military movements as we had learned, although we did not have a gun.

It was now a full company of 106 men, rank and file; as fine a body of men, according to numbers, as ever tendered their services, their lives and their swords to monarch, sovereign or commonwealth. The enlistments had been made not only from the Mountain, Portersville and Covington, but from Mt. Zion, Randolph, Mason and Stanton. They came from school-room, from college, from the farm, the counting-room and the workshop.

I recall the names of twenty who were college graduates or came direct from college to the company. There were perhaps more. There were two ministers of the gospel and at least one theological student, W.H. Price. The great bulk of the company was young men between the ages of twenty and twenty-five. Two of our members W.M. Carnes and Holmes Cummins, if the test had been applied, had not reached the legal age of enlistment—eighteen years. There were four married men (two of them, J.W. Winford and Debro Slaughter) were discharged at the camp of instruction at Union City, and I overlooked their names and stated at the unveiling the number was only two in all. There were three widowers, two of them without families. A member of the company, who had reached thirty years, passed among us as an elderly man, entitled to great respect and to have first choice at all soft snaps. Among these was Ed Jones whom we made company commissary. The boys played a practical joke on him occasionally, but they never resented his red hot reprimands and fierce abuse.

On the 6th of May 1861, Tennessee seceded. There was then no longer any apprehension about arms being supplied etc., for forthwith came the call for volunteers and we tendered our services to the governor immediately, asked to be sworn in and armed at once. After some days came an order to report to the camp of organization at Jackson, Tenn., on May 22, 1861. The intervening time we passed in camp Clopton hardening up our muscles by daily drilling, and when off duty engaged in running, jumping and other athletic sports and entertaining our lady friends when they visited us, which was quite often.

The ladies of the county at an expense of forty dollars purchased material which their deft fingers converted into a beautiful Confederate flag to be presented to us on the eve of our departure, which was fixed for the afternoon of May 21, 1861. This was to be a memorable occasion. Nothing like it had ever been seen in Tipton county. Miss Mollie D. Thompson, at one time a teacher in the Tipton Female Seminary, had been selected by the ladies to make the presentation. Well knowing her patriotism, her skill in composition, her grace of person and manner, our captain was more troubled about his reply than he would have been about arranging the details of a battle. He procured a copy of her address in advance and turned it over to Junius Hall and myself to frame a fitting reply, which we did in the highest style of the art known to us. When we read it to the captain, he was not as loud in his praise as we expected, but he took it graciously. Later he informed us that he could not memorize our lofty expressions, and such as he could remember would not fit in his mouth. The fact is, like a sensible man as he always was he had determined to be himself and make his response in his own way. A great crowd was in attendance, sorrowful but proud mothers and sisters, venerable fathers who fein would take their boys' place, proud of them as they could be, but their hearts trembling for the uncertain fate that awaited them. Major Morgan of Covington, who appeared to me one of the most princely men I ever saw, was in evidence, as well as all the old men who took an interest in organizing the company, and many more.

We did some of the best drilling we were capable of. About 11 o'clock we marched in front of the stand erected for Miss Thompson's convenience, and in a tender touching, but firm voice she addressed us and very gracefully presented the flag.

The sentiments she expressed were loudly applauded. I have that address before me now. Of course some of the hopes she fondly indulged were never realized, but the address is interesting now. When quiet was restored, our captain responded in a very gallant and chivalrous manner, acquitting himself quite to the satisfaction of the whole company, and June Hall and myself observed with satisfaction that the captain in the midst his ardor wove in unconsciously one or two at least of our high flown phrases which, in our judgment, gave luster to his sensible and patriotic speech like diamonds on a kingly crown.

When Capt. Wood had responded to Miss Thompson and accepted the flag at her hands, he turned to our stalwart ensign-elect, Wm. Young, who looked brave enough and strong enough to

thresh a whole Yankee regiment himself, and said, "I now place it
in the hands of our noble and heroic color bearer." Here handing
him the flag, he continued, "Take this standard and protect and
defend it as you would your life; unfurl it to the breeze, and may it
wave and wave on forever until nations shall learn war no more." I
think I never saw a man look so brave as Ensign Bill Young did
just then. There were no Yankees near and there were any number
of beautiful and admiring women looking proudly at him. Ensign
Young took Capt. Wood's oratory in a very literal sense and he
proceeded then and there to unfurl the flag and wave it, too. This
was a sort of climax. The cymbals clashed, the drum beat and a
shout went up. Mr. Ensign Young, as he bravely waved the beautiful flag, seemed to us and everybody at Clopton to be about the
biggest man in the Confederacy, and we all felt a little disappointed
that each one of us had not been elected ensign; but realizing that
we all could not be color-bearers, we silently swore that we would
defend the flag even more bravely than the man who bore it. I give
the reader here the presentation address of Miss Thompson and
Capt. Wood's gallant reply:

Southern Confederates—The scene before us is one of no common interest. The fathers, sons and brothers of this people are
here in military array to receive our strongest and perhaps last
testimonial of our esteem. You now go forth to battle for your homes
and your firesides, for your liberty and these defenseless ones.
You bid adieu to your kindred, and sever the dearest ties of nature, to fight for your country, but you go in a just cause, and the
God of battles will be with you.

The flag, too, while it now sends a thrill of martial pride through
every heart, is at the same time calculated to produce reflections,
as it takes the place of that of our once glorious and now degraded
union; that under which our forefathers fought and which we have
so long delighted to honor; that union which has sent abroad vast
stores of wealth and scattered far and wide religious and political
wisdom. But its knell has sounded, its glory has forever departed,
and the time has arrived when the two sections must sever their
bands which can no longer be held by unnatural interest and friend-
ship.

Northern fanaticism would place on us a yoke more oppressive
than that of Great Britain. Denying our independence as a nation,
they would have the wealth of the South to enrich their northern
coffers. Forgetting we are brethren, they would send bloodshed
and devastation throughout the land. They care not for the widows' tears; the cry of the orphan and the oppressed is unheeded.
Totally void of every principle of honor, "They would uproar the

universal peace, confound all unity on earth" to subjugate us. But this will be a harder task to prove than has perhaps been imagined. 'Tis true they have the advantage in weapons for warfare, but we have strong arms and brave hearts that will spill the last drop of blood in defense of our liberty. Subjugate the South! As we might they undertake to stop the current of the mighty ocean as to conquer Southern sons with their bloodthirsty minions. Our mothers have instilled within us a different principle. Our freedom was given us by God Himself, and rather than live in bondage we will die in the struggle for independence. This is a time to try men's souls and women's too; an era unequaled in the annals of history. Let every true patriot arm himself for the contest, and in the battlefield be assured lies our only safe protection. There is the place to guard your homes. Though you leave your families sad and desolate, the duty you are about to perform is to them as well as your country. A duty the neglect of which would be sufficient to debase you from the kingdom of grace and glory, and render you a reproach to your family and a traitor to the land that gave you birth. The time is here for immediate action. The perfidy of the North has deceived us long enough. Where are now our Northern men of Southern principles? All vanished! "Let us be up and doing with a heart for any fate." Ours is a just cause, a conflict forced upon us. Forget not Him who alone can give us victory.

We would congratulate you, Capt. Wood, on your noble company who so promptly offered their services. Formed as it is of the chivalry, intelligence, refinement and piety of our land, you have every reason to be hopeful. You go with a band of pure hearts, actuated alone by principles of equity, justice and liberty. "What stronger breast-plate than a heart unstained? Thrice is he armed who hath his quarrel just." Go, then, in the strength of Israel's God to conquer and contest, "knowing the race is not to the swift nor the battle to the strong." Women's prayers will unceasingly attend you. She can not fight in the field, but she will importune heaven in your behalf and will ever be happy to be engaged in works of love and mercy for the soldiers of her land. Without a murmur she will see her husband and sons join in this warfare, with no assurance of seeing them again, but she will pray for your safe and speedy return, when this shall be an independent and happy nation; and should you die on the battlefield, she "knows you die no felon's death, but a warrior's weapon frees a warrior's soul."

And now, Capt. Wood, permit me in behalf of the rest of my sex, to present you and your gallant band this flag as a testimonial of our admiration, heartfelt gratitude and entire confidence in your undertaking. May it never be trailed in the dust, but be borne triumphantly in every battle. Unfurl it to the breeze, and may it in-

The First National Pattern Flag presented to Captain Wood and the
Southern Confederates at Clopton's Campground.

Clopton's Campground
The training ground of the "Southern Confederates" and later
Company G of the 51st Tennessee and Company B of the 7th
Tennessee Cavalry.

spire you with fresh courage, and incite others to join you in this holy cause. May the time soon come when the influence of our Southern Confederacy shall be felt from ocean to ocean, when it shall be the admiration of all nations and the oppressed of every land shall seek its protection. And when at last this flag has been shredded by the elements may your names be handed down through future generations as your country's honor and your nation's glory.

And when you come to pass from earth away, whether amid the din of battle or in your own peaceful homes, may you, when you stand in the twilight of two worlds, be enabled to look back on this as the greatest act of your life, and may it suffice to obliterate from God's book of justice all your past offenses. God grant you may return safely to your kindred crowned with laurels of victory; but should you not be permitted to meet them again on earth, they will have the consolation of knowing you died in a great, a glorious and a just cause, and 'tis our sincere prayer to Almighty God that you may join hands on the shining shores of heaven and bask forever in the eternal sunshine of liberty, where wars are forgotten and peace is perfected, God bless you, gentlemen.

Capt. Wood's Reply.

Miss Thompson and the ladies whom you represent—I wish very briefly to express for myself and company our heartfelt appreciation of the exhibition we have witnessed here today. We are indeed in the midst of a crisis. The rights, equality and justice for which our fathers fought have been denied us, our overtures for peace and justice have been treated with contempt; our arguments and entreaties have been met with insults, and we are now menaced with invasion. There is no alternative left us but to meet the fanatic on the battlefield and teach him a lesson which he has refused to learn in Washington City. It does not become us here to boast of valor yet to be shown, of deeds of daring yet to be performed, for the Bible says to those who are putting on the armor not to boast as those who put it off; but it would be strange indeed if our hearts should lack courage or our arms want nerve when we are thus so warmly encouraged by such a host of fair women and brave men.

The noble part which you and the dear ladies you represent have taken in this great cause is enough to encourage the patriot's heart, enough to mottle with the blush of shame the coward's cheek. We go then with fresh zeal to engage in the cause we have espoused, and allow me to say that I haven't one single doubt as to the final result of this conflict. The States already seceded can bring 50,000 heroes, and more if necessary, into the field. These men, aroused with the true spirit of chivalry and patriotism, incensed by the perfidy and treachery of Abe Lincoln, led on by the gallant Davis, and battling for their homes and firesides, will be invincible by any force the enemy can bring against them.

Miss Thompson, you alluded to the stars and stripes. You have well said its glory has departed. It is a venerated thing of the past. It was glorious when borne by hands of patriots and heroes, but when on the 5th of last March it was placed in the hands of Abraham and from being the banner of liberty and equality it changed into a badge of tyranny and oppression, it became contemptible and disgusting in the eyes of every patriot. We therefore discard it forever and accept this as the standard of our country. Under its folds we will rally and drive back the Northern invaders from our soil. We accept it as the highest mark of consideration which you can confer on us, we accept it as a sacred trust which we promise to defend with our lives, our fortunes and our sacred honor. I now place it in the hands of our heroic color-bearer. Take this standard and protect it and defend it as you would your life. Unfurl it to the breeze, and may it wave and wave on until nations shall learn war no more.

Miss Thompson, we appreciate every word you have spoken to us today. May you who have spoken so kindly to us and all the dear ladies who have by works and labors of love encouraged our hearts and strengthened our hands, may you live long to grace the land of your nativity, the joyous pride of the sunny South; may you live long to nerve the patriot's arm and encourage his desponding spirit, and if we meet no more here, may we one and all shake hands on the banks of Deliverance, where the wicked cease from troubling and the weary are at rest. Ladies, I thank you.

After all, William Young, so proud of the trust committed to him, never had an opportunity to wave it as color bearer in presence of the enemy. Dan Calhoun, as already stated, died while we were in the camp of instruction at Union City, and William Young was elected to the very responsible post of orderly sergeant in his place. After the speech making and the cheering there was some quick step marching under our new banner and then, "Break ranks, march!" to give opportunity for our last dinner at Clopton and a chance to say farewell.

Whatever other soldierly accomplishments might have been wanting to the gallant "Southern Confederates" because of the lack of having seen service, they had at least magnificent appetites and could get away with rations quite as successfully as the most experienced veterans. During the first month of service at Clopton, we had lived on the fat of the land—that is, when Commissary

Jones[2] would let us. All provisions sent to camp were turned over
to his care and keeping. In the midst of the greatest profusion he
tried to introduce a strict economy that would have well become
the later days of the Confederacy. That is to say, he locked up the
boiled hams, the odorous roast lamb, the chicken and turkey, pies
and cakes, and from the remnants of the last meal he sheared together bits of ham and chunks of beef, potatoes, onions, pies, pick-
les, chicken, cornbread, light bread, etc., stirred and boiled and so
made a grand hash which the boys denominated "cush." This stern
old commissary used to swear by all the gods in the catalogue of
false deities that not one of us should have a single bite to eat but
"cush;" that it was a part of a soldier's duty to learn economy and
especially learn to eat anything; he reminded us every day that ere
long we would be delighted to have food far less palatable than his
cush; he insisted it was the best hash ever made and used to gulp
it down himself by the big spoonful to encourage us to partake.
There was universal rebellion, however, and peace generally was
only restored at last by the stern old commissary unlocking the
boxes of hams, cakes, etc. At the last dinner at Clopton the old
commissary even was toned down and became gentle and did not
mar the occasion by his everlasting and universal pot of "cush." It
was rather a sad dinner. We were proud of our company and fond
of our friends. We put on a little of the swaggering air as we thought
soldiers ought to do; we rallied our friends, we joked and laughed,
but somehow the jokes were flat and our laughter sounded hollow
and dismal. We munched over the most tempting viands, for we
found that somehow the mouthfuls stuck in our throats. After dinner in all the shady nooks were little family groups; mother had
sought opportunity to speak a last word to her dear boy, to give
him a Bible, a kiss and her blessing. She could not trust herself to
the general farewell in public; she knew she would break down,
and by a sort of tacit understanding no tears were to be shed that
day. "God bless and protect you, my dear boy, and restore you to
these arms again, but whatever your fate, let me always hear that
under all circumstances you did your duty and did it well," were
the final words that greeted my ear, and a like message every mother
present gave her boy that day. It is perfectly astonishing how brave
and self possessed they were. There were other sweet, sad fare-
wells in sequestered nooks about and around the sacred bill. Little
parties, each soldier boy with his lassie, strolled hither and thither;
they walked gaily enough, but there was an air of unwelcome sad-
ness which refused to be banished. In the friendly, inviting shade
vows of everlasting constancy where plighted and lips that never
had met before touched in the last farewell, and the transport of

such parting seemed rich compensation for years of toil, hardship and danger to come. The photographer at old Bloomington had been rushed with business, and tiny little lockets were in great demand. But now the time of departure was at hand. A great train of wagons was drawn up. Rev. D. H. Cummings,[3] pastor of the Presbyterian church at Covington, known now to every member of the company and the personal friend of most of us before and who had held services in camp for us the two Sunday evenings preceding, invoked the protection of the God of battles for us and earnestly prayed his blessing upon our cause. Orderly Sergeant Calhoun was busily engaged in distributing the boys in the numerous wagons, forming company, so to speak, by wagons. In the first wagon he deposited Ensign Young with the banner, attended by a volunteer guard of honor. I have said we had no arms. I should have said except knives. All the color guard and nearly every member of

Thomas Jefferson Walker July 4, 1842–August 30, 1920 One of the few original members of Company C who were present at the surrender at Greensboro, North Carolina.

the company were armed with huge knives, which were carried in a sheath like a sword—a real barbaric, bloodthirsty weapon, made by an ingenious blacksmith, Bill Ward. Later on they were put to the ignominious service of cutting bread and chopping up tough beef instead of drawing blood from the treacherous foes of our dear country. We had no knapsacks and each soldier packed up his small belongings as best he could. These consisted of his blanket, a change of undergarments, his Bible and keepsakes, an occasional book of light literature, but more likely some history of Napoleon, or Cromwell's wars, or perhaps of Frederick the Great, a pencil or fountain pen, note paper and envelopes, and all the literary inclined had huge rolls of foolscap or a large blank book to keep a diary, which the possessor fancied would be an authentic history of the war when the last gun should be fired. How many diaries were there started during the way I do not know, but precious few of them ever amounted to more than a few dull pages.

Good thoughtful old Commissary Jones was loading up boxes of ham, pies and other provisions to regale us by the way and sustain us at Jackson till we were sufficiently in touch with the state to "draw rations." When Orderly Calhoun had seen everything loaded and taken his seat in the first wagon, the drivers tightened up their lines, cracked their whips and away drove the gallant Southern Confederates from the presence of father, mother, brothers, sisters, sweethearts, neighbors and friends, and with their prayers and blessings following them. Away they drove to their unknown fates, to discharge the highest duties of a citizen, the defense of native land. Away they drove where honor beckoned, where fame offered an imperishable name, but God of mercy protect them, for they drove where pestilence lurks, where death crouches in their pathway. They were to become a part of the army of Tennessee and whenever the armies under Polk, Bragg, the Johnsons, Beauregard and Hood sent up a shout of victory, their voices joined the proud huzzah; in all the great battles of the West—Shiloh, Perryville, Murfreesboro, Missionary Ridge, Chickamauga, the campaigning in Georgia, the battles of Franklin and Nashville—some of these boys were to be found among the wounded that strewed the track of battle and among the pale-faced dead on all these battle-swept fields were found the stiffened corpses of brave and lamented members of this gallant company, and at last, when the last roll was called at Greensboro, N.C., a battle-scarred remnant, still preserving the autonomy of the company—the first company Tipton gave to the defense of the South—answered proudly to their names.

Noble, gallant band of patriots, accomplished soldiers, first to respond to the call of arms, proud am I to have been associated with you.

CHAPTER 3

A HISTORY OF COMPANY C, 9TH TENNESSEE REGIMENT, FROM ITS ORGANIZATION IN 1861 TO THE SURRENDER, 1865
by Captain James I. Hall

Besides the names mentioned by Charles B. Simonton as being subscribers to the fund for equipping the Company, Mr. Robt. Sanford and Col. Wm. Ligen were preeminent. My recollection is that my father, J. D. Hall, Robt. W. Sanford, J. D. Calhoun, John E. Stitt & Wm. Ligen subscribed and paid each $500.[1] The larger part of the remainder of the $5000 was raised in the Mountain neighborhood.[2] Our people were not secessionists but were ready to give themselves and their money to defend their homes. The organization of the company began in my school on Monday morning after the proclamation of Lincoln calling upon the state for troops.

When I went to the school house,[3] I found the larger boys debating the question of quitting the school and entering the Southern Army. I neither encouraged nor attempted to dissuade them from it. I told them however that if they were going to the war, I would go with them and stay with them to the end. This promise I kept but very few of them came back.

The names of the members of Company C who were at that time or had been pupils of the Mountain Academy under my charge were—W. N. Carnes, G. C. Calhoun, J. W. Calhoun, J. H. Cummins, E. O. Chambers, J. B. Daniels, E. T. Elam, J. C. Elam, W. H. Foster, J. W. Gee, J. L. Hall, J. Green Hall, J. W. Lemmon, H. C. McQuistion, R. A. Marshall, J. W. Strong and Bailey Sanford. Quite a number from the school joined other companies then and afterwards. In all eighteen boys went directly from the school to the ranks. The high moral character of the men composing the company brought to us recruits from the country for miles around. So we had in our company the very best material. A large majority were mature men. The boys did not go out until the next year.

The committee of which Capt. Wood[4] and I were members, [were] appointed to procure materials for uniforms—could find nothing suitable of sufficient quality except gray jeans. The suits were made by the ladies, the brass buttons were furnished by "Uncle Henry Morrison" who had been fortunate enough to secure about a peck of them twenty five years before at an auction.

I was not in good health when I joined the company. [I] had a chill at the camp ground which detained me at home several days after the company had gone into camp at Jackson [TN]. I remember that I carried with me a bottle of brandy and a bottle of Hostettiers Bitters, believing them to be necessary to my health. I soon learned that I would be better without spirits and shortly after entering the camp, signed a pledge of total abstinence from all intoxicating liquors during the war. I did this mainly because it was represented to me that my example might have a good influence upon some of the young men in the company who were in danger of forming bad habits. This pledge was entered into by a majority of the company and so faithfully kept that I remember on several occasions during the war, rations of whiskey issued to our company were either poured out or given away. On my arrival at Jackson, I found that our company had not gone into any regiment. The organization of the 9th regiment was delayed for more than a week by what seemed to me unseeming and unpatriotic greed for Regimental office on the part of some of the company officers of other companies, not of ours. We were kindly and hospitably treated by the citizens of Jackson while we were in camp there. The ladies of Jackson notably Mrs. Dr. Jackson, visited our camp almost every day and gave our men lessons in cooking that were very much needed. For instance, the men were taught not to put navy beans in boiling water. At that stage of our campaign, we had a great abundance of commissary supplies of all kinds. Pork, beans, hard bread, sugar & coffee supplemented by boxes from home containing all the delicacies that our mothers, sisters and wives could provide. Gabe, my servant, was cook for my mess and was by no means an expert. I remember on one occasion when Dr. Jackson was to be our guest. I was afraid to trust Gabe and made the biscuits myself with results by no means satisfactory. Dr. Jackson furnished proof of his gentle birth and good breeding by eating them with apparent relish. During the first year of the war, while we were within reach of some supplies of good things from home, [they] were so abundant that we made little use of regular commissary supplies and wasted great quantities of wholesome provisions that in the after years of the war we would have rejoiced to get. I have seen whole barrels of pickled pork thrown out on the ground. When Columbus [KY] was evacuated in the Spring of 1862, our company commissary Ed Jones had among other commissary stores, several packs of coffee which the men had not wanted to draw. These he sent home by consent of the company to his family and friends.

After the formation of the regiment, we were ordered to the camp of instruction at Union City, [TN][5] where we spent two months drilling and where we received our arms. There, measles broke out among the soldiers and we had our first experience in nursing the sick. While in camp there, the soldiers were visited by their lady friends, their mothers, wives, sisters & children. Cousin Mattie Wood came to visit Captain Wood bringing with her, Louis, her little boy and my two little girls. It was a holiday time for all—children as well [as] grown people. On the 4th of July, there was a grand dance and picnic dinner. At Union City, the 6th & 9th Tennessee Regiments[6] with Polk's Battery attached, were formed into a brigade under command of Brigadier General Benjamin F. Cheatham.[7] This was Cheatham's old brigade. Sometime during the next weeks at Columbus, Colonel H. C. King's Kentucky battalion[8] was temporarily attached to the brigade. After remaining at Union City two or three months, we were ordered to New Madrid, Mo. The baggage in [the] charge of some of the officers was sent by rail to Memphis and from there by the river to New Madrid. The army marched across the country to Tiptonville by way of Reelfoot Lake. Capt. Wood went with the baggage and I was left in command of the company. The weather was excessively hot and the march was particularly tiresome to our company from the fact that then as always afterwards, we formed the rear guard and had the duty of bringing up the stragglers. At Tiptonville we took [a] boat for New Madrid. A considerable army was collected there under command of Gen. Leonidias Polk.[9] I do not remember exactly how long we remained there. For some reason that I do not know, the camp at New Madrid was broken up suddenly and the army conveyed in boats down the river as far as Randolph.[10] We stayed there only one day and were carried back on the boats to Hickman, Ky. where we were landed. From that place, we were conveyed (by railroad) to Columbus which place we occupied early in the fall of '61.

Not long after our occupation of Columbus, the battle of Belmont[11] was fought on the opposite side of the river from our camp. Gen.

Grant, with a large force came down from Cairo in boats and attacked an Arkansas Regt. which was stationed there. This was our first experience of the roar of artillery. Two brigades were sent over under the command of Gen. Pillow to the assistance of our troops. A sharp fight ensued in which Gen. Grant and his troops were driven from the field and forced to take refuge under cover of their gun boats. Our troops were conveyed across the river in steam boats. Our brigade did not cross over, consequently, were not engaged in the battle though we were in line the whole time ready to be sent over if we were needed. Very effective work was done in the battle by a large gun which we had put in position in our works only a day or two before. After the firing of two or three shots, a ball became lodged in the gun and in attempting two days after, to discharge it, the gun burst and the magazine exploded thereby killing the gunner and seriously injuring Gen. Polk who was directing the firing of the gun.[12]

Very soon after the battle of Belmont, our company was detached from the regiment and assigned to guard duty in the ordnance department under the bluff in the town of Columbus. We remained there until after Christmas. At that time quite a number of our friends from home visited us and brought with them abundant supplies of good things from home—sausage and spare ribs & other things which were wanting in our camp fare.

Soon after Christmas, we were returned to the regiment and went into permanent winter quarters on the bluff. We built snug and warm cabins and passed the winter very comfortably in them. Ours was a double box house.[13] Capt. Wood and I occupying one room, Lieutenants Simonton & Lemmon, the other. We were undisturbed in our position during the winter. Nothing of special interest occurred to relieve the monotony of camp life. We had no regimental chaplin but kept up a weekly prayer meeting and attended services on Sunday held by Lieut. Witherspoon of the 6th Tenn. Regt.[14]

After the reorganization, Lieut. Witherspoon was made brigade Chaplin. He was a devoutly pious man and a wonderfully attractive preacher. He died the following winter at Shelbyville, Tenn. in the midst of a great revival which he was conducting among the soldiers at that place.

Before leaving Columbus, we learned of the fall of Forts Henry & Donelson.[15] Of course I felt great anxiety about the fate of my brothers John & Henry[16] who were there. John was captured and taken to Johnson's Island—Henry escaped. After the fall of these forts, our position at Columbus was no longer tenable. Toward the latter part of March, Columbus was evacuated and our troops withdrew by way of the Mobile & Ohio Railroad first to Humboldt where we went into camp and remained for more than a week. I got [a] leave of absence for several days and went home for the first time. I remember when my furlough came. I was so worn out with marching that I felt as if I could not walk a step farther. When that came—felt that I could walk the whole way home—had an uncomfortable ride on the top of a freight car from Humboldt to Mason, the journey consuming the whole night and part of a day. I spent several days very pleasantly at home. After my return to the company, we were carried down the road on cars to Corinth, Miss. This was just before the battle of Shiloh.[17] After remaining several days in Corinth, we were marched back about 20 miles to Bethel Station on the Mobile and Ohio Railroad. Here, the army was organized for the attack on General Grant's forces at Pittsburg Landing. While here, I was informed of the serious illness of my brother Henry at Corinth and got leave to go to him. I remained with him until his death which occurred March 30th, 1862.

During my stay of a few days at home, the battle of Shiloh occurred. Right here I want to note a change Providence (wrought) in connection with that battle. While in camp at Columbus, for want of other employment, the men and officers, many of them had both acquired a fondness for gambling, a game called "chuck a luck" played by throwing dice from a tin box, was the favorite game. An old lady who came into camp to visit her son and had been kept awake all night by the rattling of the dice in the tin box in which was so constant that she mistook that sound for that of a coffee mill, expressed her sympathy for the soldiers next morning by saying that she felt very sorry for their having to grind coffee all night long. After breaking up our winter quarters, the mania for gambling took another form; cock fighting. As we marched down toward Corinth, the whole country was scoured in the search for fighting birds and whenever the army would halt in their march a crowd of soldiers would collect to witness a cock fight. The throng was so thick sometimes that men on the outskirts of the crowd would climb up into trees to get a better view. There were five or six men mostly officers, who were ringleaders in this sport. In the battle of Shiloh, they were all killed and although I remained in the army three years after this, I do not remember ever seeing or hearing of another cockfight in our Regiment or in fact, in any part of the army with which I was there in. When I returned to the army after the battle of Shiloh, I found the regiment again in camp at Corinth— Our company had suffered heavily in the battle. Our wounded had been sent to the hospital. Many of the men in camp were sick from exposure and fatigue during the battle. It rained almost incessantly and our camp was a mud hole. Our drinking water was procured from a branch in which I remember seeing a dead horse lying. It was here that the reorganization of the army took place. Lieut. Simonton was elected Captain of the Company. I still retained the place of First Lieutenant, Robert Lemmon,[18] a Lieutenant of our company, being left out in the reorganization of the company, volunteered as a private soldier in the ranks, although on account of a crippled hand, he was not subject to military duty. We remained in camp or in our fortifications at Corinth for six weeks or more awaiting the approach of the enemy from Pittsburgh's Landing. At the end of this time, the enemy who had been approaching very slowly and cautiously (eighteen miles in six weeks) appeared before our works. It was expected that a battle would take place here but for some cause which I do not know, our works were evacuated and our army retired to Tupelo, Mississippi. As usual in such cases, our regiment formed the rear guard in the retreat.

I remember on the night march in this retreat that I was so overcome from want of sleep and fatigue that I went to sleep while marching in column and was awakened by running against the man before me when the column halted. Our camp at Tupelo was [a] pleasant relief from the horrors of camp life at Corinth. We had [a] pleasant camping ground and good water. Our sick men here rapidly regained their health and strength. Upon the whole, I have very pleasant recollections of our short stay at Tupelo—had no sickness except a few cases of measles among new recruits.

While we were at Tupelo, Bob Gibbs, a boy of eighteen years of age came to me and asked for my influence with the Colonel of the regiment for his appointment to the office of color bearer in the regiment. Our color bearer had been killed in the battle of Shiloh and as it was a very dangerous and responsible position, it did not seem to be one that a boy would seek. I had been drawn toward young Gibbs while we were in winter quarters at Columbus. By coming in upon him at night, he was holding prayers with his mess composed of men, all much older than himself and none of them except himself, professing of religion. Only he wanted the standard bearer's place. I represented to him that it was the most dangerous position in the line and that there was a strong probability of his being killed in the first battle we might go into. His reply was that he had thought of all that and that he did not volunteer with the expectation of shirking dangerous duty. I advised him to consider the matter a day or two longer. At the expiration of that time, he came saying that he still wanted the place. When I presented his application to Colonel Buford, he objected, that Gibbs was too young to be trusted with the colors. I assured the Colonel that he need have no hesitation on that score and [I] related to him the incident mentioned above as occurring in our camp at Columbus. His reply was: "If he's that sort of a boy, he will do". Poor fellow, my forebodings with regard to his fate were realized a few weeks later in the battle of Perryville. He was shot through the heart and instantly killed while bearing his flag in front of the regiment.

From Tupelo, our army was transferred by way of the Mobile and Ohio Railroad to Mobile and from there by rail to Chattanooga by way of Montgomery, Ala. and Atlanta, Ga. Our regiment had lost heavily in the battle of Shiloh and had been to a small extent weakened by desertion after our homes fell within the Federal lines. So that when we were marching through the streets of Mobile, our number did not seem so great as that of some of the other regiments and some of the good citizens of Mobile were inclined to make sport of our weakness. A man standing on the sidewalk called to one of the boys asking what regiment that was. The reply was "Ninth Tennessee". The next question was "What makes your regiment so small?" The reply to this was: "Stranger, we went into the

Ensign Robert H. Gibbs
A clerk on a riverboat before the war, he was killed at Perryville, Kentucky while carrying the Standard in front of the regiment.

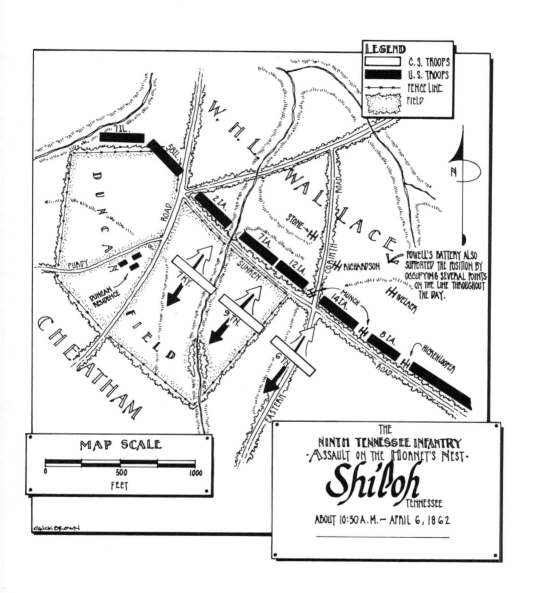

LEGEND

C.S. TROOPS
U.S. TROOPS
FENCE LINE
FIELD

7 IL.
58 IL.
2 IA.
7 IA.
12 IA.
STONE
RICHARDSON
MUNCH
14 TA.
WELKER
8 IA.
HICKENLOOPER

W. H. L. WALLACE

DUNCAN FIELD

PURDY

DUNCAN RESIDENCE

CHEATHAM

ROAD

SUNKEN

CORINTH ROAD

7 KY.

9TH

6TH

EASTERN

ROAD

N

POWELL'S BATTERY ALSO
SUPPORTED THE POSITION BY
OCCUPYING SEVERAL POINTS
ON THE LINE THROUGHOUT
THE DAY.

MAP SCALE

0   500   1000
FEET

THE
NINTH TENNESSEE INFANTRY
·ASSAULT ON THE HORNET'S NEST·
Shiloh
TENNESSEE
ABOUT 10:30 A.M. — APRIL 6, 1862

CHUCK BROWN

battle of Shiloh with over a thousand men and while we were lying
down in reserve, an Alabama regiment in front of us stampeded,
ran over us and killed one half of our mess". This was so near the
truth that no further questions were asked. We remained at Chattanooga several weeks. Our regiment was encamped about four
miles south of the town on what had been the home of Ross—Chief
of the Cherokee Indians, a beautiful place. We did not know the
plans of General Bragg but learned afterwards that he was organizing for the Kentucky Campaign. Our stay at Chattanooga was very
pleasant, our duty [was] light as the country abounded in supplies. We had the opportunity of buying vegetables and fruits—
things we had not been able to procure anywhere else. We had
preaching in camp and I attended service once or twice on Sunday
at the Presbyterian Church in Chattanooga of which Reverend Mr.
McCalla was then Pastor. I remember how sweet the sound of female voices was to my ear in the congregational singing. This was
our first experience of a mountainous country. Most of our West
Tennessee men had never seen a mountain before.

After remaining here a month or more, our regiment was conveyed by a steamboat twenty miles up the Tennessee river to a
little place called Harrison. Here we were put ashore and entered
upon the memorable campaign into Kentucky. Our first experience of mountain climbing was crossing Walden's Ridge. This we
accomplished without great fatigue and encamped a day or two at
Pikeville in Sequatchie Valley. Our next march was across the
Cumberland Mountain. On account of the extreme heat of the
weather and great scarcity of water on the mountain, we were compelled to make this march in the night. We filled our canteens with
water late in the afternoon and reached the top of the mountain
before sunset. [We] marched all night and arrived at the foot of the
mountain on the other side near Sparta about sunrise next morning having marched a distance of about twenty five miles during
the night. Here our wagon trains failed to make their appearance.
Consequently we were out of rations. I was offered a dollar for one
biscuit that I was fortunate enough to have, but as I could not eat
the dollar, I preferred the biscuit. General Cheatham came to our
relief by buying a field of corn just in good roasting ear stage and
the fence enclosing the field for fuel to roast the corn. The boys
were so hungry that some of them ate from six to eight ears of
roasted corn a piece. After remaining at Sparta for several days, we
continued our march Northward across the Cumberland River which
we forded at Gainesbourgh to Tompkinsville, Kentucky where we
halted for several days.

Our next march was to Glasgow, Kentucky where we halted again and remained for a few days. While at Glasgow, we had the privilege of attending a communion service at the Presbyterian Church of which the Reverend Mr. Forman was Pastor. This was the first communion service we had had the privilege of attending since we joined the army and it was to us, a very impressive service. The Sunday we were at Glasgow, an attack was made by a Mississippi Brigade under command of General Chalmers,[19] on a fort twenty miles away at Munfordsville[20] on the Louisville & Nashville Railroad. As the fort, which was supposed to contain a small body of troops had been heavily reinforced, our troops were repulsed with heavy loss. The fort was situated near the south bank of [the] Green River on low grounds. The north bank of the river was a high bluff which overhung the village and the fort. On the second night after the above mentioned repulse of our forces, our whole army was moved around by a circuitous route and put in position of the bluff. We did not reach this position until about three o'clock in the morning. We were ordered to lie down and sleep until daylight and be in readiness then to make an assault on the fort. When I awoke the next morning, the sun was more than an hour high and I thought that our forces had failed. General Bragg had stationed a hundred guns during the night on the bluff directly overlooking the fort so that after daylight when the enemy had discovered our position and numbers, they, at the summons of General Bragg, surrendered the fort. I must confess that I was well satisfied with the event as I was not hankering after glory that morning. From Munfordsville, our march was continued up the Louisville & Nashville Railroad towards Louisville until about nightfall when we were halted and counter marched back towards Munfordsville. It was a dreary march. The rain pouring in torrents almost the whole night. The reason of this movement was a false report of a large body of the enemy's troops moving in our rear near Mammoth Cave.

The next morning, we left the railroad and marched across the country a distance of sixty miles in two days to Bardstown where we remained in camp several days and recruited. Here we were getting into the "bluegrass" region and had [a] great abundance of supplies. The beef particularly was fat and tender—so fat indeed that our men quarreled for the lean parts. Our march to this point had been through a well matured country abounding in springs and running water. But after entering the bluegrass country, we suffered for the want even of drinking water. The only water accessible was pond water and that, warm and muddy. The water we were compelled to drink was so muddy that we could not wash our faces in it. The weather was very hot and dry which made the dust on the turnpikes intolerable. The army was kept under very strict discipline during this campaign. Men were not allowed to straggle or commit depredations on private property. I remember one occasion as we were passing a large orchard heavily loaded with tempting apples, the owner came galloping up to our Colonel with the request that he would turn his regiment into the orchard. The Colonel thanked him but told him that it was against orders. He went to the Brigade Commander, General Cheatham, where he received the same reply. So we had to pass on by without getting an apple. I was fortunate enough to have with me my man, George, the best forager in the army, who had no conscientious scruples about disobeying orders in this line. I supplied him with money and this way always got the best [the] country afforded. While we were in camp at Bardstown, our men had the privilege of buying supplies from the farmers around.

While six of us were lying dangerously wounded under a temporary shelter at Perryville, one of our men, Tom Melton, gave us his experience in foraging at Bardstown somewhat in this way: "Boys, there's one thing I have never done. I have never stolen anything. The other day when we were at Bardstown, Emory Sweet and I went out into the country foraging. We came to a place that seemed to be entirely deserted, found some delicious grapes and ate all that we wanted. After eating the grapes, we were about to start back to camp when an old goose, the only living thing on the place, came waddling in sight. The temptation to have goose for supper was very strong so we ran it down and I caught it. Just then, I thought to myself: Tom Melton, have you lived an honest life to this time and are you now going to break your record by stealing a goose? Boys, I could not do it. I turned that old goose loose, but the fact was, she was a mighty poor old goose."

From Bardstown, we moved through Lebanon, Perryville & Danville to Harrodsburg. The night before passing Danville, we camped near a fine spring, this being the first water we had had for several days that was fit to drink. In passing by Danville, we came in sight of old "Centre College" where I had been in school fifteen years before. Junius Hall & I could not resist the temptation to slip out of ranks and lie down on the grass in the college campus. While lying there, we heard General Cheatham expostulating with one of our fellow officers, an old Centre College boy, for leaving his command without orders. Fortunately for us, we escaped his notice and quietly regained our places in lines.[21]

We found more Southern sympathizers in Harrodsburg than at any other place on our march thus far. Our men were very ragged and dirty but this did not prevent their being kindly and hospitably

treated by the people of Harrodsburg. Our camp in Harrodsburg
was near a noted spring at which it was said Daniel Boone rescued
his captive daughter from the Indians. After a stay of two or three
days here, we were marched back directly to Perryville[22] while the
forces of the enemy under General Buell[23] were concentrating. This
march was made in the early part of the night. After a few hours
sleep, we were formed into [a] line of battle early in the morning.
All the forenoon of that day, October 8th and part of the afternoon,
were spent in shifting our position and arranging the line of battle.
There was occasional firing throughout the day between our advanced line and that of the enemy. I suppose it must have been
about three o'clock in the afternoon when our division, under General Cheatham, which occupied the extreme right of the army in
our advance toward the front, came upon a large body of Federal
troops strongly posted on a hilltop. Directly on top of the hill was
stationed a battery of six guns which kept up an incessant fire and
did great execution among our men as they advanced to the attack. I remember that our advance up the hill was hindered by a
worm fence, the corners of which were grown up thick with brushes
and briars. This fence had to be let down in some places to enable
our officers to ride through. We lost a good many men here. After
crossing the fence, our advance was up a steep incline until we
reached a point where we could look down the muzzles of the
enemy's guns which were stationed just over the crest of the hill.
Colonel John W. Buford[24] had been severely wounded at the fence
and was compelled to retire from the field. The command then dis-
solved upon Major G.W. Kelso[25] whose horse was shot in attempting to cross this same fence. It was a very valuable horse [which]
had cost him five hundred dollars a few days before and Kelso
thought it would be prudent for him to take the horse to the rear
for treatment. This left us without Regimental officers, so that the
left was the first to discover the position of the battery and a heavy
line of infantry in its rear. At this point in our advance, we were
brought under the fire of the battery not fifty feet in front of us and
of the infantry line in its rear. Their fire was terrific and we were
losing men rapidly; so much so that it caused our line to falter its
advance. Just here, I heard Captain Irby's[26] ringing voice: "Lieutenant Hall, here's the battery in our front—pass the order down
the line—let us make a charge and take it". This was immediately
done. We went forward with a yell and in less time almost than it
takes to tell it, the battery was ours and the infantry supporting it
[was] driven from the field. I am more particular about making this
statement because credit of the capture of these guns was afterwards claimed by the First Tennessee Regiment of our brigade and

the name of this regiment was inscribed on one of the guns, which
is now at Nashville. But I know this: Companies "C" & "D" of the
9th regiment were directly in front of the guns and from the position that Captain Irby of Company "D" and I occupied in our advance, we could look down in the throats of the guns. Besides, as
we advanced past the guns in pursuit of the infantry, two of our
men (Gladney McCreight and Tim Carnes) were wounded while firing upon the retreating enemy from the shelter of the gun car-
riages, our company passing right over the ground occupied by the
guns. The enemy, after retreating half a mile or more through a
bluegrass pasture, reformed their line of battle in a very strong
position. The nature of the ground I do not know, because I never
reached it. While we were forming the line for a second charge,
which also was successful, I was shot through the body with a
minie ball. This shot was not particularly painful, but came with
such force as to knock me down. It was there, about five o'clock in
the evening, I fell on the grass in a beautiful bluegrass pasture.
Some of the boys lifted me and placed me under the shade of a
tree. The column advanced to the attack and I was left alone. James
Lemmon, John William Calhoun and other boys of my company
offered to carry me off the field but I felt that there were others who
needed assistance more than I did. Very soon I heard a terrific
volley of musketry in the direction our men [which told me they]
were advancing, followed immediately by the "Rebel Yell", which
told me that the enemy were retreating and our boys pursuing.
The firing became more and more distant when finally it ceased
almost entirely. Our men had driven the enemy for more than two
miles. As the route by which our troops had advanced in pursuit of
the enemy was somewhat circuitous, our Hospital Corps, in bearing the wounded to our field hospital in the rear, did not pass over
the ground where I was lying. So that I was left entirely alone until
the firing ceased and some of the boys who knew where I was lying
came back to pick me up. I had seen no [one] during all this time
except a Mississippian who came by, taking a prisoner to the rear.
The shadow of the tree had shifted so as to leave me exposed to the
sun. When he saw me lying in this position, he ordered his prisoner to climb up into the tree and cut down some branches. As the
Mississippian carried the gun, this order was very promptly obeyed.
They arranged a nice bed for me in a shady place, laid me carefully
on it and then went on their way to the rear. I had lost a good deal
of blood and consequently was very much weakened and had not a
very distinct recollection of how I was taken from the field. I remember being carried for a short distance by John William Calhoun
on his back. I think he must have been carrying me from the out of

the way place where I was lying to the road where the ambulances were passing.

I remember being carried on an ambulance down the dry bed of a creek. It seemed to me for a long, long distance. Our hospital camp was located on what was called the "Goodnight" farm.[27] It must have been nearly midnight before we reached the hospital. The surgeons, on examination, pronounced my wound necessarily mortal and I was placed on the ground under an apple tree between two men whose wounds were similar to mine. A liberal dose of morphine was given to each one of us and I remember its soothing effect on me. The other two men were suffering intensely from their wounds and knowing that my wound was similar to theirs, kept me awake for a long time by asking me such questions as "how I felt", and "whether I thought I could last through the night". I finally got to sleep and when I awoke the next morning, I had a corpse at each elbow. The men had died while I slept. Contrary to the predictions of the surgeons, I was still alive. After staying here a day or two with five members of my company—Archie Baird, George McDill, James Peter Holmes, John Hanna and Tom Melton, I was placed under a temporary shelter constructed of boards and old planks found lying about the place. The night after the battle, General Bragg withdrew his troops from the field toward Harrodsburg. I did not know anything of this until the next day when the Yankee troops came into our camp. We realized that we were prisoners inside of the Yankee lines. Our men were very destitute of clothing—most of them having no clothing except what they were wearing. Many of the wounded had their clothes cut off them by the surgeons who dressed their wounds and in this way lost a great part of the little clothing they had. Rations of good quality were furnished to us in abundance by the Federals, but we were not supplied with clothing or shelter.

After a few days, the good women of Kentucky came into our camp and supplied us as far as they could with such things as we needed. Among others, I remember particularly the good Mrs. Hogue, the wife of the Presbyterian minister at Lebanon, Ky. who was untiring in her efforts to add to the comfort of our boys. Besides being a good woman, she was an outspoken "Rebel". Captain Simonton was also wounded and was somewhere in the camp but I did not see him. Of the five men above mentioned in the shelter with me, two, Archie Baird had a broken thigh and Tom Melton who had a comparatively slight flesh wound, died. Three of us, James P. Holmes and George McDill, who was shot through the lungs and pronounced mortally wounded, and I, have lived to be old men. John Green Hall, Robert Lemmon & Willie Holmes re-

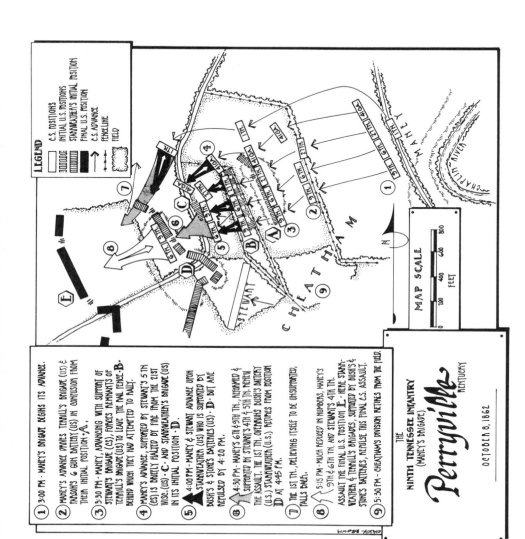

LEGEND

- ▢ C.S. POSITIONS
- ▨ INITIAL U.S. POSITIONS
- ▨ STANNWEATHER'S INITIAL POSITION
- ■ FINAL U.S. POSITION
- →↑ C.S. ADVANCE
- ⌇ FENCELINE
- ▨ FIELD

MAP SCALE

0   200   400   600   800
FEET

THE
NINTH TENNESSEE INFANTRY
(MANEY'S BRIGADE)

Perryville
KENTUCKY

OCTOBER 8, 1862

① 3:00 PM - MANEY'S BRIGADE BEGINS ITS ADVANCE.

② MANEY'S ADVANCE MOVES TERRILL'S BRIGADE (US) & PARSON'S 6 GUN BATTERY (US) IN CONFUSION FROM THEIR INITIAL POSITION - **A**.

③ 3:30 PM - MANEY, ADVANCING WITH SUPPORT OF STEWART'S BRIGADE (C.S.), FORCES REMNANTS OF TERRILL'S BRIGADE (US) TO LEAVE THE RAIL FENCE - **B** - BEHIND WHICH THEY HAD ATTEMPTED TO RALLY.

④ MANEY'S ADVANCE, SUPPORTED BY STEWART'S 5 TH (CS) IS BRIEFLY HALTED BY FIRE FROM THE 21ST WISC. (US) - **C** - AND STANNWEATHER'S BRIGADE (US) IN ITS INITIAL POSITION - **D**.

⑤ 4:00 PM - MANEY & STEWART ADVANCE UPON STANNWEATHER (US) WHO IS SUPPORTED BY BUSH'S & STONE'S BATTERIES (US) - **D** - BUT ARE REPULSED BY 4:20 PM.

⑥ 4:30 PM - MANEY'S 6TH & 9TH TN. REFORMED & SUPPORTED BY STEWART'S 4TH & 5TH TN. RENEW THE ASSAULT. THE 1ST TN. OVERRUNS BUSH'S BATTERY (U.S.) STANNWEATHER (U.S.) RETIRES FROM POSITION **D** AT 4:45 PM.

⑦ THE 1ST TN, BELIEVING ITSELF TO BE UNSUPPORTED, FALLS BACK.

⑧ 5:15 PM - MUCH REDUCED IN NUMBERS, MANEY'S 9TH & 6TH TN. AND STEWART'S 4TH TN. ASSAULT THE FINAL U.S. POSITION - **E** - HERE STANN- WEATHER & TERRILL'S BRIGADES, SUPPORTED BY BUSH'S & STONE'S BATTERIES, REPULSE THIS FINAL C.S. ASSAULT.

⑨ 5:30 PM - CHEATHAM'S DIVISION RETIRES FROM THE FIELD.

CHUCK BROWN

mained to nurse the wounded. The people from the country around were in our hospital every day. One day a man came along whom I recognized as "Big Jim Harlan" whom I had known as a boy fifteen years before at Danville. I had concealed under my blanket a Maynard Rifle, which I had bought for Will Carnes, at Chattanooga— the regular army musket being too heavy for a boy of his age and size to carry.[28] As he was wounded in this battle and captured, he had sent me the rifle to take care of. After renewing my acquaintance with Harlan, and finding him to be a good Rebel, I asked him to take charge of the gun until I should call for it. He kindly consented to do this and secured it in the voluminous folds of a big Yankee overcoat that he was wearing. Twenty nine years afterward, while walking along the streets of Danville, I ran upon a man whom I immediately recognized by his colossal proportions as my quondam friend. After making myself known, I asked him if he remembered taking charge of the gun. His reply was "why yes, I've got it out at home now just waiting for you. Do you want it"? I told him that I would like to have it so he brought it in to me the next day with the remark: "There's a cartridge belt and some cartridges lying about the house somewhere that I couldn't lay my hands on this morning but never mind, I'll have them ready for you when you come back again". After I had remained in the hospital about two weeks, my kind friend, Colonel Joshua Barbee of Danville, who was a Union man, sent his carriage for me and took me to his house. Here I was placed in the room which I had occupied fifteen years earlier while a student at Centre College and was treated with unremitting kindness by Colonel B. and his family. Not more than a day or two after my removal from the hospital, a heavy snow fell greatly to the discomfort of our men in the hospital, since they weren't all provided with shelter and clothing. A large number of our men, however, were taken to the homes of the good people in the country in Harrodsburg and in Danville. Willie Holmes and James Peter were cared for at the house of Mr. Messick in Danville where Willie met with Miss Moore whom he afterwards married. I had lost all my clothing except what I had on in the battle of Perryville. Mrs. Barbee with characteristic kindness supplied all my needs.

By the way, Mrs. B. was a sister of General Speed Smith Fry of the Federal army who killed General Zollicoffer.[29] I met General Fry at her house and learned from him the particulars of the killing. As he (General Fry) and his staff were ascending a steep hill in a heavy rain, on nearing the summit, they discovered a party of Confederate officers ascending the opposite slope. Both parties, on account of the rain, were wearing waterproof coats which concealed com-

**Brigadier General
Speed Smith Fry
4th Kentucky
Infantry, U.S.A.**

**Fry shot and killed
Brigadier General Felix
K. Zollicoffer at the
battle of Mill Springs,
Kentucky on January
19, 1862.**

pletely their badges of rank. On account of the abruptness of the
ascent on both sides of the hill, neither party was aware of the
approach of the other until they were within buckshot range of
each other. Both parties immediately began firing with the result
that General Zollicoffer was killed by a bullet from General Fry's
pistol. General Fry expressed great regret at the occurrence on
account of his high regard personally for General Zollicoffer. From
my knowledge of General Fry's character, I have no doubt of the
truth of his statement. Quite a number of my old friends, even
among the Union men, came to see me and treated me with the
greatest kindness. Dr. Lewis Green, then President of Centre College, and Mr. McKnight, one of the professors were particularly
kind. Among the ladies who were most kind to me were Mrs. Talbot, Miss Fannie Barbee, Miss Sallie Barbee and Mrs. Vest, wife of
George Vest who had been a college mate of mine and was then a
member of the Confederate Congress. These were all outspoken
rebels. I want to mention the fact that Mr. Barbee, although a pronounced Union man, in befriending and sheltering me, was in danger of bringing suspicion on his loyalty.

As I have said before, my wound had been pronounced mortal
and besides one of the squad who were left behind on the night of

the battle to bury the dead reported the next morning at Harrodsburg, that he had assisted in burying me. Consequently [I was] in the list of the casualties of the battle of Perryville. I was reported in the Southern papers "mortally wounded, twice dead". This was the first news my people at home had of the battle. As the report was official and seemed to be entirely reliable, my father & mother and friends at home supposed it to be true and had no hope of ever seeing me again. The only one who seemed inclined to discredit the report was my little six year old daughter who could not be convinced that I was dead and would say to her grand-mother: "Grandma, Papa's not dead. He'll come home one of these days, now you'll see". When I finally reached home, arriving there in the dusk of evening, I found her standing alone on the porch—seemingly waiting for me. Her greeting was: "why here's Papa", and then to her Aunt Sarah, "I told you, he would come back". James Peter Holmes had also been reported mortally wounded and was at this time lying at Danville. My father and Dr. Holmes prevailed upon Mr. Cyrus Johnson of Memphis who was a Union man and could get a passport through the lines to go to Danville for the purpose of looking after James Peter and bringing my body back home. When Mr. Johnson reached Danville, to his surprise, he found that we were both alive and that I was sufficiently recovered from my wound to meet him at the door. This was about a month after the battle. The money he brought to defray the expenses of my removal was gladly received as I was in need of clothing.

I remained at Mr. Barbee's a little more than two months before I was sufficiently recovered to be removed. Sometime in December, Mr. Barbee, when on a business trip to Louisville, met with my old friend and collegemate—Dr. Lapsley McKee, Pastor of [the] Presby-terian Church in Louisville. When he learned from Mr. B. that I was at his house and wanted a parole, he sent a message to me to come down to Louisville and that he would do what he could for me. As Dr. McKee was a strong Union man, he of course, had influ-ence with the Federal authorities. While I was preparing to go to Louisville, and accept his kind offer of assistance, my old friend and former pastor, Rev. D. H. Cummings of Covington, who had a passport by reason of being a Mason, came to Danville to try what Masonry could do with the authorities. He was successful in get-ting passports for Willie & James Peter Homes, George McDill and myself to Louisville. We left Danville on Saturday and spent Sun-day at the house of Mr. Moore, father of the lady whom Willie Holmes afterward married. Previous to this, I had made a trip in company with Mrs. Talbot and Miss Sallie Barbee to Harrodsburg for the purpose of visiting our wounded who were being cared for by the good people of that town. On this trip, I met my man George, who supposing that I was dead, had remained at Harrodsburg and had found employment as cook in the Yankee Army. When he learned that I was trying to get back home, he begged me to take him with me. My meeting with him was accidental, as I was passing in front of a livery stable, I saw him at the rear end of the building, beckoning to me and trying to attract my attention. He told me that he had been watching me all day seeking an opportunity to talk with me privately that if the Yankees knew that I was his master, they would not let him go back with me as that would be a return to slavery. When I met him afterwards on the same day on the street, he did not recognize me and acted toward me as if I were an entire stranger. He remained at Harrodsburg and I saw him no more until the Monday morning when we started from Harrodsburg to Louisville. Just as we were starting, he, having been on the lookout for us, climbed upon the outside of the stage. I managed to pay his fare without exciting suspicion. When we reached Louisville, we took rooms on the same floor of the Galt House. George managed to smuggle himself into my room and remained there during the whole of our stay in the city. On the morning after our arrival, Mr. Cummins went out to look up Dr. McKee. He also visited the headquarters of General Boyle who was commander of the Department.[30] On his return, Dr. McKee accompanied him. I was truly glad to meet with an old friend whom I had not seen for fifteen years and he seemed equally glad to meet with me. After spending a little while in talking over old times and reviving the pleasant recollections of our college days, he asked what he could do for me. I told him that if it was possible, I wanted a parole for myself and three of my company—two of whom, George McDill and James P. Holmes, seemed to be past all hope of recovery. His reply was: "I can get it. General Boyle is under obligations to me and said to me some time ago, Dr. McKee, if you ever want anything from me, ask for it and you can get it. I have never had occasion thus far to ask anything of him and it affords me great pleasure to make this the first favor asked".

Dr. McKee then went with Mr. Cummins to General Boyle's headquarters and with the aid of the former's influence & the latter's Masonry, our paroles were obtained. In the afternoon, I made a very pleasant call on Dr. McKee at his study. There, I met Mrs. McKee whom I had formerly known as Miss Sarah Speake—daughter of the gentleman with whom I boarded during my first session at college. From Louisville, we came by steamboat to Fulton, Tennessee. I do not remember any incident worthy of mention on this trip except that James Peter Holmes and George McDill were so much exhausted by the trip that we feared they would not survive it. We were so fortunate as to meet with some of our neighbors at Fulton and in this way secured conveyance home. As for my part, I went out with Uncle Alsues Hall who happened to be there on horseback, both [of us] riding the same horse. As I was a soldier and entitled to special honor, he insisted upon my taking the saddle. I was rejoiced to be at home once more after an absence of nearly twelve months. As my parole was binding until there should be an exchange of prisoners, I remained at home until July, 1863 when I was notified of a general exchange of prisoners and was directed by our authorities to rejoin my command. Our part of Tennessee was in a very unsettled state. Memphis, Jackson, Fort Pillow and other strategic ports were occupied by Federal garrisons. In Tipton County, there were no Federal troops stationed and this fact made our country a safe refuge for bands of irregular Confederate cavalry troops who came in to forage and to recruit. Whenever it was known to the Federal authorities that any considerable body of these men were within their lines, troops would be sent out from Fort Pillow or Memphis to capture these forces or drive them away. Sometime in April (1863), Colonel Richardson came into the country with his regiment of Confederate cavalry and established his

**Reverend David Hayes
Cummings
1813–1873**

Born in Pennsylvania, he traveled south while working for the American Tract Society. He was the pastor of Mt. Carmel Church until 1850 when he moved to pastor the Covington Presbyterian Church. Utilizing his Masonic standing, he traveled north during the war, in order to rescue Captain Hall, Sergeant Willie Holmes and Privates James Peter Holmes and George McDill from Yankee captivity.

camp near Colonel Stitt's place in our immediate neighborhood.[31] A Federal force of cavalry and artillery under [the] command of Colonel Grierson was sent from La Grange to drive Richardson out. A slight skirmish took place in which several men were killed. Richardson, in his flight with a few of his men, came through my father's place. Some of the balls fired by the troops pursuing Richardson, struck my father's house. This was the first experience that our people had of the ravages of war. The Federal troops, besides doing other damage, took every horse and mule off my father's place not even leaving unbroken colts. While the Yankees were plundering the place, Richardson and his men escaped. Considering my parole a safeguard, I made no effort to escape. Much to my surprise and discomfiture, I was arrested and carried off to Memphis with the prisoners captured from Richardson's band. We were taken in wagons through the country by a circuitous route to La Grange, Tennessee where we were put aboard the cars and sent to Memphis.

On our arrival at Memphis, we were marched to the Irving Block[32]—the military prison of the post. My experience here was far from agreeable. The prison was the place of confinement for the most desperate characters, mainly from their own army. Such a band of thieves and cutthroats, I hope never to fall in with again. At the head of the stairs down which we were marched into the underground prison, we saw lying the body of a man, who had a few minutes before, been stabbed to death in the prison. The room in which we were confined was about 150 feet in length and 25 or 30 in width and so closely crowded that it was difficult to find a place to sit on the floor during the day or to lie down at night. Our party, consisting of twenty five or thirty men, taking warning from the sight of the dead man lying at the head of the stairs, took timely precautions to protect ourselves against the thieves and thugs who were carrying on their work of robbery and theft without any interference on the part of the guard. A man who had been knocked down and robbed applied to a guard standing by for protection. The reply of the guard was: "It is not my business to protect you in here, but to keep you from getting out". Our little party made our way through this mob in a compact body to the farther end of the prison, where we took position against the wall which afforded us protection from the rear. Of course, we had no weapons except our pocket knives many of which were taken from our men. When my time came to be searched for weapons by the officer of the guard, I handed to him a small tortoise shell pen knife the property of my little daughter, Mary Eliza, which I happened to have in my pocket when I was arrested and carried off. When I explained to him that the knife was the property of my little girl and that I was very loath to part with it, he very generously gave it back to me. For the first night or two, we kept men on guard for our protection but did not find it necessary to continue this long. The roughs, soon finding that we were banded together for mutual help, left us alone. Of our whole body, not one was molested while during the two weeks that I was in prison. I do not think that a single man, committed to the prison during that time, escaped being garroted and robbed. We gradually became accustomed to this state of affairs, and strange as it may seem, to a great extent indifferent. It was about this time that General Grant issued his famous order against Jews, who were following his army for the purpose of buying cotton. I remember seeing a number of Jews who were arrested under this order and brought into the prison without exception. They were knocked down and robbed and I must confess that I did not feel much sympathy for them as they were willfully violating their oaths of allegiance and General Grant's express orders. We had food in abundance but very coarse in character and wretchedly served. The bread, hardtack, was brought in on a tray and was not distributed but scrambled for by the mob. Sometimes the tray was overturned and the bread spilled on the floor. The meat, fried bacon sides, was brought in a wooden bucket and every man helped himself with his hands. Sometimes the meat, wet with the sauce, just as the bread, and was spilled on the floor but more was wasted. Coffee was served in tin cans. I was indebted to my young friend, Tom Norwent for what I got of the prison fare as he did my scrambling for me.[33] I was fortunate enough to have a little pocket money and succeeded in getting my meals from a restaurant outside of the prison which I shared with my friend, Norwent. He had been in my school at the Mountain and was particularly kind and helpful to me during my imprisonment. The condition of affairs in this prison was simply horrible, still we made the best of it and passed the time more agreeably than one would imagine under such circumstances. After I had been confined here about two weeks, my friend, a Mr. H. T. Lemmon of the city, learned of my imprisonment and immediately interested himself with the authorities to secure my release. I was required to give a bond of ten thousand dollars, to be forfeited on condition that I would not report to the authorities in Memphis before returning to my command. Mr. Lemmon & Mr. Tom Gale very kindly signed the bond and so I secured my release. My kind friend, Mr. Lemmon, very generously furnished me with a horse to take me home. This horse was also carried off by a Federal raid soon after my return home. I remained at home without experiencing any incident of special interest until sometime in July. After the fall of Vicksburg, I then received notice of a general exchange of prisoners and an order to rejoin my command immediately. As there was no special difficulty in passing the Federal lines, I might have gone through at once to my command which was at Chattanooga. I was restrained from doing this, however, by the bond I had given to report in Memphis before my return to the army. Had I not done so, the bond would have been declared forfeited and my friends compelled to pay the ten thousand dollars. This was what the Federal authorities expected and hoped would be done when they required the bond to be given. I was now in a dilemma. If I surrendered myself to the Federal authorities, I would necessarily become their prisoner again. If I did not, my friends would suffer. In this trouble, my old friend, Rev. D. H. Cummin[g]s, with his usual kindness, came to my assistance. He went with me to Raleigh and there induced Mr. Sam Allen, a citizen of Raleigh who had a passport through the Federal lines, to go into Memphis, state my case to the authorities and ask them to surrender the bond. This they refused to do and directed me to report in person to them. After going back home and remaining a few days, I went down to Memphis and reported to the Provost Marshal.

As he did not know what to do with me, he ordered me to report to General Grant at Vicksburg and gave me an order for transportation to that place. I asked permission to see the friends who had been so kind to me in the city. This request, they refused and ordered me to go immediately on board the boat.

I made the trip to Vicksburg on a Federal transport crowded with Federal soldiers—do not remember anything of special interest on this trip except that I was treated with uniform kindness and courtesy by the Federal soldiers aboard the boat. I arrived in Vicksburg too late in the evening to report at General Grant's headquarters, which was a little way[s] out of town. The Provost Marshal of Vicksburg kindly invited me to supper and gave me a place to sleep in his office. After taking breakfast with him the next morning, I reported to the Provost Marshal General of the Army at General Grant's headquarters. I stated my case and asked him what he would do with me. His reply was that as I had voluntarily come inside their lines after being exchanged, he would be compelled to consider me a prisoner of war and would deal with me accordingly. I insisted that I had the assurance of the Federal authorities in Memphis that if I would surrender myself to them, I would be sent through to my command. He finally consented to refer my case to General Grant (whose tent was within a few steps of us) and ordered me to report again the next morning. When I came back the next morning he said to me: "General Grant has ordered you to be sent through to your command but if I had my way with you, I would have sent you north to prison". I told him that General Grant had done just what I expected he would do and that I was glad that he, the Provost Marshal, had not had his way. This was an act of simple justice on the part of General Grant, still, I have always felt grateful to him for it and have always regarded him as a just and honorable man. I was furnished transportation to New Orleans and ordered to report to General Banks. This was about two weeks after the surrender of Vicksburg and regular service by boat between that place and New Orleans had not been established. On this account, I was detained at Vicksburg nearly two weeks waiting for a boat. On the morning of my first day here, after my visit to General Grant's headquarters, I made some inquiries in regard to a boarding place. I was directed to the house of a Mrs. Kane, a resident of the place and a red hot rebel. When I reached her house, I met a Federal officer at the door. On inquiring where I could find Mrs. Kane, he directed me through the hall to the dining room. When I reached the dining room door, on looking in, I saw a large room occupied by two or three long dining tables extending the entire length of the room, crowded with her boarders—Federal officers who were there eating dinner. I sent a message by a servant to Mrs. Kane who was at the farther end of the room, that I wanted to see her. On receiving this message, she called to me in a loud tone, that she had no time to come to me and that if I had any business with her, I must speak it out. I told her that I had called to make arrangements with her for board for a day or two, but before you decide, said I, whether to take me or not, I had better let you know who I am. I am a Rebel soldier, belonging to Bragg's Army, was wounded and captured at Perryville, and am now on my way to my command. Her reply was: "You will do, but you will be in mighty bad company with all these Yankees". This caused considerable merriment at the table and when dinner was over, quite a number of the boarders came up to me, introduced themselves and treated me with the greatest cordiality and I must say that during the whole time of my stay of about two weeks with these men, I received nothing but the kindest and most courteous treatment from them. Most of them were surgeons, connected with the hospital service of the army—some of them in charge of the Confederate sick and wounded who were too ill to be removed when the place was captured. Among them were some men of more than ordinary culture and refinement. A Doctor Bryan, a professor of the Jefferson Medical School of Philadelphia and a Dr. Cushman of Quincy, Ill., a Virginian by birth who although a Union man and in the Federal army, had a deep sympathy for the people of the

South. The kindness of these two men in particular contributed to make my detention in Vicksburg as pleasant as it could be under the circumstances. While here, I had a striking illustration of the feeling of Northern men toward the so called Union men of the South. One evening while a party of us, seated on the porch, were enjoying the cool evening breeze, I, being the only one of the party who was not a Federal soldier, a man came in from the country on business with General Grant and as he was detained overnight, wanted lodging at Mrs. Kane's house. Taking a seat with us on the porch and wishing to make himself agreeable to the party, he soon volunteered the information that he was a staunch Union man and had always been one—boasted how he had kept out of the Confederate Army first by one plea and then by another up to that time. As I was in citizen's dress, he did not suspect that I was a Confederate soldier. After he had finished his recital, old Dr. Bryan turned to me saying: "Captain, is this man a fair specimen of your Southern Chivalry?" I replied to him: "No, Doctor, he is your man. We don't claim him". There upon, there broke loose up on him such a volley of abuse that he was completely dumbfounded. He found difficulty in answering the question, why, if he was such a good Union man he did not shoulder his musket and go and fight for the Union. He seemed to be puzzled and did not understand why I, a confessed Rebel, should be courteously treated while he, a professed Union man should be vilified and abused.

Just then, very opportunely for him, the supper bell rang and we all went into supper leaving him on the porch. He didn't want any supper. When we returned to the porch after supper, he was gone in search of more congenial company which he would hardly find among good soldiers on either side.

Before going farther, I wish to say, that while a prisoner, I can recall no instance of ill treatment on the part of any army officer or private in the regular service. On the contrary, I can recall many acts of kindness which unexpected on my part, but none the less grateful to me. At the end of the two weeks, I found a boat going down the river as far as Baton Rouge. I took passage on this boat, arrived at Baton Rouge in the early part of the night [and] went to a boarding house kept by a lady (a recent convert from secession to unionism). After getting breakfast, I left her house and went downtown to the old hotel which was not kept open then except on the sly, for the accommodation of Rebel soldiers. Here I met with two or three old Rebs and we passed the day very quietly and pleasantly together. I got the best of everything procurable without money and without price. Late in the afternoon, I took passage on another boat for New Orleans, which place I reached early the next morning. On this boat, I made the acquaintance of several citizens of New Orleans who were good Southern men. I remember that when the boat landed at the levee, I asked a gentleman standing beside me on the guards where I could get some good chewing tobacco. He pointed out a house opposite the landing saying that he thought they kept good tobacco there. When the boat landed, he went ashore but I remained on board until General Banks sent a guard to escort me to his headquarters in the St. Charles Hotel. On my way, I I requested the guard to take me past the house that had been pointed out to me. When I went in and inquired whether they had any good tobacco, the merchant handed me a large package of tobacco neatly wrapped with the remark: "no charge, already paid for". I will remark in passing that this was the only time during my whole trip that I was treated as a prisoner and escorted by a guard. On reporting to General Banks, I was furnished with transportation to Pascagoula and given the liberty of the town while I should remain in New Orleans. Here I had an opportunity of witnessing the loyalty of the citizens to the Southern cause. The Federal rule in the city at the time was of the most despotic character. Banks had succeeded Butler and was not much improvement over the "Beast". The best citizens of the place, old men and ladies, were being banished from the place daily. Any open expression of sympathy for the Southern cause subjected the party to immediate banishment. Notwithstanding this, I remember that as I walked along the street in my Confederate uniform, men would beckon to me from their business houses and upon my going in would inquire whether I was in want of anything and whether they could help me in any way. Fortunately, I was in no need of help but felt mighty grateful to them for their kind intentions.

In the afternoon, after procuring some bread and cheese, I went aboard a schooner lying at the New Basin bound for Pascagoula. We were towed down the canal to Lake Pontchartrain where the sails were unfurled and we started on our voyage. This was my first and so far my only experience of a sailing vessel and of being entirely out of sight of land, which occurred both on the lake and on the gulf. My fellow voyagers consisted almost exclusively of citizens of New Orleans—old men and ladies who were being sent outside the Federal lines as registered enemies. As these people were all Creoles and somewhat exclusive, I found very little acquaintance with them. In fact I was so unfortunate as to be suspected by them of being a spy. A young Confederate soldier, a former resident of the city of New Orleans and an Englishman by birth, happened to be going out on the same vessel. As he had some intimacy with these people, he learned their suspicions in regard to me and apprised me of the state of affairs. These good people had been warned that a Federal spy would go out with them and they knew everyone else except me. [They] very naturally concluded that I was the man. My young English friend who knew the man they suspected me to be, was not entirely successful in convincing them of their mistake.

When we arrived at Pascagoula and reported to the Confederate Provost Marshal, my young friend pointed out a man to me, who seemed to be on very intimate terms with the Confederate official as the man for whom I had been mistaken. Now here was a strange state of affairs. A Yankee spy, seemingly enjoying the confidence of the chief man of the post—he had come over the day before. When we left the office, my comrade asked my advice as to whether he should reveal the trice character of this man to the Provost. We both agreed that as he seemed to be on such intimate terms with our authorities, that it would not be safe for him to report him as a spy. Some months later while with my command, I received a letter from my English friend saying that he had been summoned as a witness before a court martial to testify against this same man who was convicted and hung as a spy. I was not free from my troubles yet. My good Creole friend, on landing, had reported me to the military commander of the post as a probable spy. When summoned before him, I had no trouble in proving from my papers that I was a Confederate soldier and had been wrongly suspected and I had no more trouble on this score.

From Pascagoula, I went forty miles across the country to Mobile, part of the way in a wagon and part on foot. From Mobile to Montgomery, Alabama, I went by steamboat up the Alabama River —had a very pleasant trip—had for company the young Englishman, whom I have mentioned before and a very pleasant young Confederate soldier who had been with us since we left New Orleans. From Montgomery, I went by way of Atlanta on the railroad to Chattanooga. Here I came up with our army, retreating from Chattanooga towards LaFayette, Georgia. During my absence from the army, my company had been consolidated with another and put in command of Captain J.V. Locke,[34] captain of the other company. I immediately took steps to have my company restored to me. As this was just on the eve of the battle of Chickamauga, I was unable to get a hearing and as I had been assigned to duty elsewhere, I had no place in line. As that (assignment lasted) until after the battle was fought, I had no regular duty in the army. Our army fell back as far as LaFayette, Georgia where we remained in camp several days. Just at this time, Longstreet's Corps was sent from Virginia to Bragg's assistance. On the arrival of reinforcements, our army moved back towards Chattanooga.

On the 19th and 20th [of] September, 1863, we encountered the enemy in the hard fought battle of Chickamauga.[35] In this battle, having as I have said before, no place in line, I accompanied our men to the field and did what I could to care for the wounded. Our company lost heavily in this battle.

After the battle, I remained about two weeks in the hospital, caring for our men while our army was besieging Chattanooga. As soon as I could get a hearing from the authorities, I pressed the claim that I had made to have my company restored to me on the retirement of Captain Simonton from service, on account of wounds received at Perryville. I became captain of the company by promotion as I have said before when I returned to the army. I found awaiting me an order to report to General Pillow for service in the rear of the army. This would have taken me entirely away from the army and from my company.

I disregarded this order and plead with Generals Maney and Cheatham that many of my company were boys—the sires of my neighbors, entrusted to my care and I was not willing to leave them and that I was physically able for duty at the front. And besides that, if the company should ever fall below the average of the other companies of the regiment in numbers, we would consent to a reconsolidation. On these claims, the consolidation was annulled and my company restored to me and I must say for their credit that it was the only single company that I know of in the army after the reorganization and consolidation of regiments and companies and although all the other companies of our regiment contained from two to three consolidated companies, ours, company C, continued until the surrender, to be the largest company in the regiment. After receiving my commission, I took charge of my company at the front. Our division was there occupying Missionary Ridge. As we belonged to the reserve corps, we were sometimes here and sometimes on Lookout Mountain until the battle of Missionary Ridge.[36]

As every school boy is familiar with the result of this battle, I will not attempt any detailed account but will only relate such facts as came under my own personal observations. Our corps, Hardee's, being the reserve corps, were encamped on Lookout Mountain at the extreme left of our lines which extended across the Chattanooga Valley to Missionary Ridge and along that ridge northward to the Tennessee River, our extreme right. This was a long, straggling line and weak from want of troops to man our trenches.

On the 23rd of November, our position was on Lookout Mountain where we had been stationed to guard against the attack of

Hooker's Corps which had crossed the Tennessee river at Bridge-
port and were encamped in easy reach of our works on the mountain. On the afternoon of this day, we heard heavy firing and saw
the smoke of battle away to our extreme right at the northern point
of Missionary Ridge. General Sherman, with his corps, had crossed
the river five miles above Chattanooga near the point of the ridge
and had taken, by assault, a commanding position on what is now
known as Sherman Heights—a beautiful suburb of the city. This
position had unfortunately been left without sufficient protection
and was captured after a mere skirmish. During the night, our
corps was marched along our lines across the Chattanooga Valley
to our extreme right on Missionary Ridge. As the march was made
in the night and hastily, our men who were on picket line in front
could not be recalled and remained on guard until the next day. As
our picket lines had been facing those of the enemy for several
days, the men on each side had become quite communicative. Quite
a lively barter trade had sprung up between the two lines—our
men swapping tobacco, of which we had an abundance, and cedar
canteens, which were quite a novelty to the Yankees for gum blankets and such things as were not procurable within our lines. I
remember that James Lemmon, who had been left behind on picket,

**Position marker of the 6th & 9th Tennessee Infantry on the first
day's battle at Chickamauga, Georgia.**

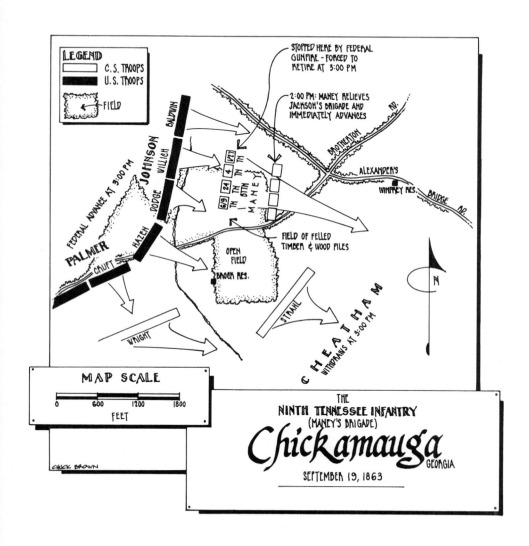

LEGEND

☐ C.S. TROOPS

■ U.S. TROOPS

▨ ← FIELD

STOPPED HERE BY FEDERAL GUNFIRE - FORCED TO RETIRE AT 3:00 PM

2:00 PM: MANEY RELIEVES JACKSON'S BRIGADE AND IMMEDIATELY ADVANCES

BROTHERTON RD.

ALEXANDER'S

WINFREY RES.

BRIDGE RD.

BALDWIN

JOHNSON

WILLICH

DODGE

FEDERAL ADVANCE AT 3:00 PM

127 TH TH TH

4 TH TH 6TH

6/9 24 TH

MANEY

HAZEN

PALMER

CRUFT

FIELD OF FELLED TIMBER & WOOD PILES

OPEN FIELD

BROCK RES.

STAHL

N

WRIGHT

C H E A T H A M

WITHDRAWS AT 3:00 PM

MAP SCALE

0   600   1200   1800

FEET

THE
NINTH TENNESSEE INFANTRY
(MANEY'S BRIGADE)

Chickamauga
GEORGIA

SEPTEMBER 19, 1863

CHUCK BROWN

when he came into the company the next morning, remarked to me: "There's going to be a big fight on Lookout today", and gave his reason for thinking so, that one of the Yankee pickets had called across to him: "Johnny, we are coming after you tomorrow and when you see us coming, get out of the way. We don't want to hurt you".

On the 24th, there was no fighting in our front, General Sherman [was] spending the day strengthening his position. Our removal from Lookout Mountain had left that part of our line almost without defenders. General Walthall was left there in command of a small body of troops. Sometime in the forenoon of this day, we heard firing in the direction of Lookout Mountain and when the fog cleared away, [we] could see the smoke of battle, not on the summit of the mountain, as that was not occupied by our troops except as a camping ground, but on the northern slope of the mountain at the Craven place where the Point Hotel is now located.[37] Hooker's Corps, on account of the weakness of our line, had no trouble in driving our men from their works who retreated up the slope of the mountain and most of them escaped capture. This was Hooker's famous "Battle Above the Clouds."[38] A most fitting appellation with the slight drawback, that it was a mere skirmish and not a battle and fought not above the clouds but in a dense fog which concealed the enemy from the view of our men until they were so close to our works with such tremendous odds in numbers, that protracted resistance was useless. After the capture of Lookout by the enemy, our men were withdrawn from the valley and put in position on Missionary Ridge. We all knew now that a great battle would be fought the next day. General Grant's plan was for General Sherman to sweep the ridge southward from his position on the north, General Hooker was to execute a singular movement from the south and while our line was being driven in from both ends, General Grant was to make an attack on our center from Chattanooga. General Sherman assaulted our works early in the morning and was repulsed with heavy loss. He, however, kept up the attack all day without success. Our brigade (Maney's) sometime in the forenoon, was sent in to relieve a Texas brigade which had been fighting all the morning. They declined to be relieved saying that it was the first time they had ever had a chance to fight the Yankees from behind breastworks and that they were rather enjoying it. We took position immediately in their rear, lay down on the ground and waited for our turn. Sometime during the afternoon, a detachment from our brigade was sent out in front of our works to drive away some Yankee sharpshooters who had [a] secure position behind a precipitous cliff. Our men, finding that they could not reach them with bullets, rolled some large rocks down the hill on them and in this way succeeded in dislodging them from their position. About four o'clock in the afternoon, we heard the fire of six guns in rapid succession in the direction of Chattanooga and we afterwards learned that these were signal guns fired from Orchard Knob by General Grant to indicate the beginning of his movement on our center. After maintaining our position on the extreme right a short distance north of the railroad tunnel until dark, we moved down south of the tunnel to the place where we had slept the night before. Our men were in excellent spirits. We knew that we had repulsed Sherman and supposed that the enemy had failed to get possession of any part of our line. Shortly after the firing of the six guns mentioned above, we had heard a brisk musketry firing which continued but a little while a short distance to our left. But we did not know at the time what it meant and were not troubling ourselves about it. After eating our supper without the slightest suspicion of what had really taken place, we lay down about nine o'clock and were preparing for a good night's rest.

About that time, an orderly came along with orders to us to move quietly and rapidly to the rear. On being asked what was the matter, he pointed out to us some bright fires burning a few hundred yards down the ridge with soldiers crowded around them cooking their suppers and said: "Do you see those fires? Those are Yankee fires and those men around them are Yankees". They had broken the center of our line and taken the ridge at General Bragg's headquarters. Several causes contributed to this disaster. After the battle of Chickamauga, the army had been reorganized. Chatham's division of Tennessee troops had been broken up and three Tennessee brigades composing it had been distributed among the other divisions. This gave Cheatham a mixed division[39] consisting of one Tennessee brigade and two from other states. This division happened to occupy that part of the line which was most fiercely attacked and unfortunately, an Alabama brigade (Day's) was not in line on top of the ridge but was in a short line of breastworks at the foot of the ridge some distance in advance of the main line. The dense undergrowth in front of these works entirely hid from their view, the movement of the Federal forces until Grant's whole army was upon them. After firing a volley, they abandoned their works and retreated up the hill toward the main line with the enemy in close pursuit.

Our line at the top of the ridge could not fire upon the enemy without killing their own men who were either in advance of the enemy or mixed up with them. Why this brigade was left in this position, I have never been able to learn. It was certainly an egregious blunder. The two other brigades belonging to Cheatham's division, being restrained from firing upon the enemy by the fear of killing their own men and having nothing else particularly to do, stampeded down the hill to the rear and thus was the famous foot race of Missionary Ridge, Tennessee. This is what is called in our school histories, the "Battle of Missionary Ridge". There was no pursuit on the part of the enemy. On receiving the orders mentioned above, our lines were immediately formed in marching order and we moved a quiet and orderly way five miles to the rear across Chickamauga Creek. Why General Grant did not pursue us that night and capture our whole army, has always been a mystery to me. That part of our line which gave way was completely demoralized, many of them having thrown away their arms in the flight. And it has always seemed to me that General Grant, by sending Sherman's force around on our flank and rear, might have bagged our whole army. We were from nine until twelve P.M.—three hours in marching these five miles as we had to cross Chickamauga creek on a railroad bridge which was a very slow process. After sleeping about three hours, our brigade (Maney's) with Gist's South Carolina brigade, were formed in line of battle facing toward the enemy whom we were momentarily expecting. We remained in this position from 3 o'clock A.M. until after sunrise. In the meantime, General Bragg, with the disorganized remnant of his army, had taken up his line of march for Dalton, Georgia some forty miles south of Chattanooga. Sometime after sunrise, the enemy appeared in sight in pursuit of our army which had been gone now more than an hour. As we had been left behind as a rear guard to protect the wagon trains in the rear of the army, we fell back slowly all day keeping in sight of the enemy. Our route of march lay across a succession of high hills with valleys interweaving. When we would reach the top of one of these hills, we could see the Yankees coming down the slope of this opposite hill which we had just crossed. Several times during the day, when too closely pressed by the enemy, we formed in line of battle and awaited their attack. They did not attack us however during this day until after sunset. The roads were very muddy and some of our wagons in the rear of the train got stuck in the mud and unless the pursuit of the enemy could be stopped, [they were] likely to be captured. To prevent this, we formed a line of battle in a very favorable position and awaited the charge of the enemy. In our front was an open field—almost a perfect level. In our rear was a thick growth of timber. The enemy charged our line through this field and were in place once for more than a half mile.[40] We poured a steady fire into them, which must have done great execution, until they were within a hundred yards of our lines. Just then a cavalry regiment, which was protecting our left flank, gave way. General Maney, seeing that we were about to be cut off, galloped down the line and ordered a retreat. In doing this, he received a severe wound in the shoulder. This occurred not ten steps from where I was standing. I did not understand General Maney's order but my men all heard it and were not slow to obey. In trying to rally them, I came upon Colonel George C. Porter of our regiment who was making for the rear as fast as his short legs could carry him and asked him what all this meant. His reply was: "It means that you'd better get out of the way as fast as you can". I took his advice and put in some of my very best running. Our two little brigades had been fighting Howard's whole corps. The delay occasioned by our resistance had saved our wagon train. The enemy directed their artillery fire down the road along which our retreat lay. To avoid danger from this, our men scattered in the woods on each side of the road. As it had now become quite dark, some time was lost in making our way through the woods, every man for himself. And in reaching our rendezvous on the farther side [of the] hill, all my company answered to their names on roll call except a young man named Anderson who was missing. He was captured by the enemy and sent to a northern prison from which he was not liberated until near the close of the war. Of course we could not know what had become of him and were agreeably surprised when he turned up safe and sound after the war was over.

Our rendezvous was at a mill on Chickamauga creek. Here, we crossed the creek on the railroad bridge. Our line of retreat during the day had been along the east side of the creek. Just here, there was a sharp bend in the creek which had made it necessary for the builders of the railroad to cross over to the west bank of the creek and about a mile and a half farther on return to the east bank, so that there was a stretch of the road about a mile and a half in length with a bridge at each end and what was supposed to be an impassable creek on the east running parallel with the road. Our wagon train had crossed the second bridge and were by this time well on their way to Ringgold, where General Bragg proposed halting for the night. The enemy were pressing us from the rear and a detachment from Hooker's corps had been sent to get possession of this second bridge. By the time that we had reformed our ranks and had gone a short distance on our march, news came that the enemy were in possession of the bridge in front and that the bridge in our rear was also in their possession. It began to look as if our time had come and that our capture was inevitable but it was not to be so. A kind Providence saved us from this fate. An old country man who was thoroughly acquainted with the roads and the creek, offered his services, to guide us along a country road to a ford on the creek. The creek had been somewhat swollen by recent rains but in an emergency like this, we felt that we must take some risk and attempt to ford it. As this was toward the last of November, the water was icy cold. Gist's South Carolina brigade was in the front, next came the battery, while our brigade brought up the rear. As the enemy were very near in our rear and to our right, General Gist, insisted that the crossing should be made as quietly and silently as possible. General Maney after receiving his wound had retired from the command of his brigade. This left Gist in command of both brigades. General Gist consequently superintended, in person, the crossing of both brigades. Right here was given a notable illustration of what some of our army officers were pleased to call insubordination of the Tennessee troops. Gist's own brigade, upon reaching the ford, were ordered to cross over with their clothes on. This order they obeyed promptly. The consequence was that they came out on the other side looking and feeling like wet dogs and were forced to make the remainder of the march with their wet clothes almost freezing on them. When our brigade came up, they were ordered by General Gist to cross in the same way. This order was as promptly ignored. Our men halted on the bank, stripped off their undergarments, made them up in compact bundles and carried them out of the reach of the water, which in the deepest part of the stream came up to their armpits, reached the farther bank without wetting their clothes, rubbed and dried themselves off, put on their clothes and felt really refreshed from their enforced bath. I was fortunate enough to avoid this experience. Colonel Buford very kindly sent his orderly back with his horse for me to ride over the stream. When I reached the farther bank, a poor fellow came up to me saying: "Mister, please lend me that horse. I have done gone and crossed over this river and left my breeches on the other side". Much as I pitied his condition, I was compelled to deny his request as the horse was not my own.

After crossing, we resumed our march, our regiment, being still in the rear. We marched until three o'clock the next morning through a broken, hilly country—sometimes through fields and sometimes through the woods. The night was clear but dark, there being no moon. This march was very fatiguing to my company as we were detailed to guard the battery. Our line of march ran parallel with the road and about fifty yards to the right of it on the side next to the enemy. The country was very rough and our march over ploughed fields, across fences and through thick woods, was very tiresome. About 3 o'clock in the morning, we came up with our army which was encamped at Ringgold, Georgia about twenty miles from Chattanooga. General Bragg was very much surprised and gratified at the news that we had come into camp. He had been apprised of our being cut off the night before and had given us up as lost. This was the most fatiguing days march that I have any recollection of. We were on our feet either in line of battle or marching from 3 o'clock of one day until the same hour of the next and I can remember that I never saw our men in better spirits and more jolly than they were in the last three hours of the march after we had crossed the river and left the enemy behind us. At Ringgold, we slept about three hours and were aroused at 6 o'clock A.M. in order to resume our march towards Dalton as the enemy were pursuing us in strong force. General Cleburne, with his Arkansas division, was detailed to protect the rear—the duty which we had performed the day before. It was a great relief to have somebody else do our fighting for us. And as Cleburne and his men were known to be good fighters, we felt no concern for our safety.

Our line of retreat lay across Chickamauga creek here again as we had had so little time for sleeping, we were the last to be aroused. As we crossed the bridge, we found Cleburne's men drawn up in line of battle on the farther side with a massed battery in position to rake the bridge when the enemy should advance upon it. We had gone but a few hundred yards beyond the bridge when we heard a terrific volley of musketry and artillery immediately in our rear. We knew that this was Cleburne paying his respects to the enemy who were following close behind us. The resistance made by Cleburne at this point was so formidable and his position so strong, that the enemy gave up pursuit and followed us no farther. This day, we straggled along through the mud until sometime after dark when we reached Dalton and were ordered to camp for the night. I had not attempted during the day to keeping my men in the ranks. They were like the rest of the army—scattered along the road. I do not think that I had any one of the company with me except John McCreight. After the order to halt, he and I looked around for a good place to sleep. After a while, we found a good hickory fire burning, which had been abandoned by the parties who built it. As the night was cold, we lay down with our feet next to the fire, lying on a single blanket and covering ourselves with another. We had now gone sixty hours with only six hours sleep and were of course very tired and sleepy. I went to sleep immediately after lying down and slept soundly the whole night until daylight, when I was awakened by a chilly feeling in my back. We had lain down on a level piece of ground with a slight depression just where we were lying. We found that we were lying in a puddle of water about an inch deep. It had been raining the greater part of the night in our faces and neither of us had been aware of it. I had been marching the last two days over stony ground or on the railroad track with a hole as large as a quarter of a dollar in the soles of both my boots, exposing my feet to the bare ground. When I attempted to put on my boots, [I] found my feet so much swollen that I could not put them on. Fortunately for me, the enemy had given up their pursuit and our army did not retreat farther. I walked in my bare feet about [a] half a mile to the place selected for our camp. Here I was fortunate enough to get a pair of old shoes that had been thrown away by one of the boys on his drawing a new pair. It was several days before I could walk with any comfort.

After remaining in our temporary camp for a week or more, our regiment went into permanent quarters in a pine forest about five miles east of Dalton.[41] This place, besides being well supplied with water, afforded abundant material for building our huts and for fuel during the winter. Having learned from our experience at Columbus, Kentucky, that it was not best to make our houses very close and warm, we built our huts close on three sides but open in front. By keeping a good fire burning in front, we managed to be moderately comfortable in the coldest weather. After finishing our quarters, we went to work at once and built a comfortable log church in which we had regular services conducted by our chaplain, Reverend Mr. McCoy of the Presbyterian Church.

After the disaster to our army at Missionary Ridge, General Bragg had resigned the command of the army and General Joseph E. Johnson[42] had been assigned to this command. General Johnson, on assuming command, had immediately adopted vigorous measures to get the army under proper discipline and control. I have mentioned above that after the battle of Chickamauga, Cheatham's division had been broken up and he, himself, assigned to a new command. Our brigade (Maney's) was assigned to General Walker's division[43] composed of one Tennessee brigade (Maney's), one South Carolina and one or more Georgia brigades. General Walker was a West Pointer and had very strict notions of discipline—not at all to the liking of our men who had been serving under Cheatham.

Very soon after we had gone into our winter quarters, General Walker organized a court martial for his division and it was generally understood that he expected a strict enforcement of military law. Very much against my wishes, I was detailed to serve on this court. In the disorganized state of our army, there had been some desertions and many violations of martial law. I happened to be the only member of the court who had ever served on [a] court martial before (I had served in the summer of 1862 in the court of

Cheatham's division at Chattanooga). This fact made me an authority in all matters pertaining to the court.

Acting on Colonel Buford's advice, by dilatory tactics, I succeeded in obstructing the action of the court so that in spite of General Walker's persistency, nothing was done. What contributed greatly to this result was the fact that our Judge Advocate was a fool. After the court had been in session some two or three weeks, the Christmas holidays coming on in the meantime, two or three of the Georgia members of the court got furloughs to go home and I was detailed on business for the regiment for more than a week. Our absence left the court without a quorum and as Walker's division was broken up before my return, I heard nothing more of it. The reason given for breaking up Cheatham's division was that it had lost very heavily in the battle of Chickamauga and as it was composed entirely of Tennessee troops, it was thought best that such a distribution should be made as would prevent a similar loss to the men of any one state. It was very strongly suspected, however by our

Private David H. Haynie Company C, 9th Tennessee Infantry
As related by Sam Watkins in his book *Co. Aytch*, during the winter encampment at Dalton, Georgia in 1864, a prayer meeting was preached by Rev. J. G. Bolton, Chaplain of the 50th Tennessee Regiment, in the camp of the 4th Tennessee Regiment. At the close of the service, ten soldiers came forward and knelt at the mourners' bench. As they were praying, a burning tree, without any warning, fell across the mourners, killing them all. One of the ten was David H. Haynie. All were buried with great pomp and splendor.

men, that Cheatham was thought to be rather too lax in the enforcement of discipline among his men.

This arrangement has worked badly. Cheatham's new division had disgraced themselves at the Battle of Missionary Ridge and the old man had the mortification of his new brigades throw down their arms on the approach of the enemy and stampede to the rear. None of his old brigades were satisfied with their new divisions and an earnest and persisted effort was made to have the old division reorganized. After some delay, this was accomplished to our great gratification. Before this was done, I remember that one day while we were in camp at Dalton, someone gave notice that General Cheatham was riding by a short distance from the camp. Immediately, a rush was made by our men to intercept him. Some of the boys ran in front to head him off. In a little while, he was surrounded by all the men of the regiment pleading with him to get us back into his division—some hugged him—some hugged his old sorrel horse around the neck. The old man cried like a child and could only say: "Boys, I'll try". After we were comfortably settled in winter quarters, having a great deal of leisure time and feeling the want of something to read, a sum of money amounting to something over one thousand dollars (Confederate money) was made up in the regiment and I was detailed to go to Montgomery, Alabama and select books for a library.

I left Dalton near the last of December for I remember that I was in Montgomery on the cold New Year's day of 1864. This being the holiday season, the hotel where I stopped, was almost entirely without servants and I could not get a fire made in my room. I sat by the office fire until bed time, then went to my room. On account of the extreme cold, I attempted to sleep without raising the window sash. I soon found that I could not do this after sleeping in the open air. I could not bear the suffocation air of a closed room. I accordingly got up, put on my clothes, even to my overcoat, raised the sash to its full height, went back to bed and had a good night's sleep notwithstanding. The temperature was down almost to zero. The fare at the hotel was just such as we had in camp—cornbread, bacon and peas except that it was a little more abundant. On Sunday morning when I came down to breakfast, suffering from a violent attack of headache, I found at my plate, a nice dish of beefsteak, one of liver and another of tripe. This was the only decent meal I had seen for six months but I was too sick to eat a mouthful of it. I succeeded in getting a fine collection of books—some two or three hundred volumes, many of them choice books. These books were generally read throughout the regiment and afforded our men both amusement and profit. When the campaign opened in the spring, the books were boxed up and sent to the rear with our extra baggage. What became of them, I do not know. We spent the winter months quietly and as far as our circumstances would allow, very pleasantly—had no drilling and had ample time for reading. It was a very cold winter. On first going into our quarters, we had made bunks around the sides of the cabins raised about two feet from the ground. Our bedding consisted of a single blanket to each man without any extras to lie on. When the weather became extremely cold, we tore down the bunks and slept on the bare ground—two men sleeping together, lying on one blanket and covering with another. Very often we would have to get up several times during the night and warm ourselves by the fire.

Our rations consisting of cornmeal and bacon and occasionally beef of poor quality were perhaps as good as the country could supply, but very scant—a ration consisting of three quarters of a pound of corn meal and one third of a pound of bacon or its equivalent in beef. General Johns[t]on's policy was to keep the men on short rations when in camp and to feed them well when on a campaign. The results showed this to be a wise policy. We had no sickness but the men were all the while hungry. Our bill of fare was cornbread and gravy for breakfast, cornbread and bacon for dinner and mush and water for supper. There was no special religious interest manifested until about the opening of the spring campaign. Still our services were well attended during the whole winter. I have neglected to mention in the proper place that when I made the trip to Montgomery, about the first of January, I stopped over in Atlanta to visit our boys in the hospital there. I found our Lieutenant, William Young, who had been wounded in the elbow at Chickamauga, in very poor health suffering as much from homesickness and disgust with hospital fare as with his wound. I saw that he would die if he remained there and prevailed upon the authorities to dismiss him from the hospital and give him into my charge. Immediately after leaving the hospital, we went to a restaurant and ordered ham and eggs. I have often heard him say since, that he never enjoyed a meal as much in his life. He went with me to Montgomery where after staying for a few days, he improved wonderfully in strength. He always said afterwards, that if he had not been removed from the hospital, he would certainly have died.

Sometime during the month of February (1864), I got a thirty day's furlough and started home. On reaching Demopolis, Alabama, I was stopped by a general order, forbidding the soldiers from our army to go farther west. General Sherman was making a raid from Vicksburg out in the direction of Meridian. It was a great disappointment to me not to be able to go on. Fortunately, I knew that Cousin Sinclair Steele lived at Macon, a few miles out of Demopolis, on the road I had just been traveling. My aunt, Mrs. Brock, formerly the wife of Uncle Minor Gracey, lived at the same place. After eating dinner at the hotel where I remember that I got a mess of turnip greens, I started back on the evening train to Macon. My aunt, whom I had once seen before, happened to be on the train. On arriving at the station, she heard me making inquiries about Cousin Sinclair and asked me who I was and whether I was related to him. On learning that I was the nephew of her first husband, she very cordially invited me to her house, promising to take me over to Cousin Sinclair's the next day. I found her husband, General Brock, a most estimable gentleman of the old school—a Virginian by birth and a man of strong wind and superior attainments. He had been Attorney General of the state of Virginia. My aunt was a woman of refinement and of great force of character. I received the kindest attention from both of them while at their house. The next day, I went to Cousin Sinclair's, whom I had not seen since I was a small boy, and received a cordial welcome from him and his estimable wife—a sister of Mrs. Brock's. Next to being at home, nothing could have been more pleasant than my stay with these good and kind people for two or three weeks. My recollections of Cousin Bettie Steel were especially pleasant.

I had been there but a few days when Cheatham's corps came down to Demopolis to make a stand against Sherman. In the meantime, Sherman, after destroying Meridian and tearing up the railroad, had gone back to Vicksburg. Our men stayed only one day at Demopolis before returning to Dalton.

Cousin Bettie took me in her carriage down to the camp with a basket of good things to eat which the boys of my company enjoyed hugely. On the whole, my stay with them was very enjoyable. A week or ten days before the expiration of my furlough, I left here and went up to Marian, near which place Cousin Sallie Hall (was Mrs. Tubbs) was living. When I reached the hotel and inquired for a conveyance to take me out to Mr. Tubbs', a gentleman standing by told me that he was Mr. Tubbs and inquired who I was. On learning that I was his wife's cousin, he greeted me very cordially and provided me a way out to his home. My coming was evidently a pleasant surprise to Cousin Sallie. She had been living away from her kinfolk among strangers since her marriage and the sight of an old friend and kinsman was most welcome. Mr. Manson Sherrill lived very near them and I spent many pleasant hours in his hospitable home and enjoyed greatly the society of his excellent family. Mr. Tubbs, I found to be a good man, kind and generous and devoted to his wife. All these people did everything in their power to make my stay agreeable for which I was grateful. On the expiration of my furlough, I returned to camp at Dalton. The change from my pleasant surroundings of the past month to the dreary and comfortless monotony of camp life was far from pleasant.

Nothing of special interest occurred after my return except that toward the last of March or first of April, General Johns[t]on had a review of the whole army in a large field. This was the only time I ever saw fifty thousand men collected in one body. A few days after, there was a sham battle. I did not witness this because I was out some seven or eight miles from the camp in charge of the picket guard though we were near enough to hear the report of the firing of the guns. A courier came out in the evening with orders and in giving an account of the sham battle, informed us that a part of the programs consisted of a cavalry charge upon the infantry in which blank cartridges were to be used. He also told us that one of the infantrymen, not liking such child's play, had chewed his wad very hard before ramming it into his gun. The consequence was that one of the charging party of cavalrymen received a severe wound in the leg. A little Dutch lieutenant, who was standing by, remarked that if it had been a real battle, he would not have been hurt at all. I relate this to show the opinion the infantry had of the cavalry. Toward the end of April, the booming of cannon was heard in the direction of Ringgold. We knew that the enemy were on the march and that the campaign had opened. Our camp was immediately broken up. All baggage that could be at all dispensed with, was sent to the rear and we were marched to the front. We knew that this was the beginning of a desperate struggle. Our number did not exceed fifty thousand men while that of the enemy was perhaps twice as great. Our division was put in a position along a precipitous ridge towards the north of Dalton, to await the coming of the enemy.

We had not long to wait before General Sherman, who had been assigned to the command of Grant's army, attacked us in force.[44] Our position was so strong that the enemy, after an ineffectual effort to take it, withdrew with considerable loss. A part of our line of fortifications consisted of a hastily constructed stone wall and several companies of our regiment were stationed behind it. The enemy had placed a battery in the valley below us about a mile and a half away. A shot fired by this battery struck this wall with such force as to knock it down for the length of a whole company. As the stones fell upon the men, they were all more or less hurt—some of them seriously. One of these men, who up to this time had been considered one of the bravest men in the regiment was so demoralized by the fight he got here, that he voluntarily shot off one of his fingers a few days afterwards with the hope of getting a discharge from the army.

General Cheatham, who happened to come along just then, called for the sharpshooters of our regiment—three men armed with Whitworth guns—and ordered them to drive away the battery. I was standing close by and watched with interest, the effect of their fire. On the first fire, we could see a commotion among the gunners. Next we saw them hitch their horses to the guns and before half a dozen rounds had been fired, they were all in full retreat to the rear. The distance was so great that I could not see whether any one had been killed but I could see that they were very badly scared.[45]

After assaulting our lines unsuccessfully for several days, General Sherman moved his army around our left flank in the direction of our rear. This necessitated the evacuation of Dalton. As usual, our regiment was left behind when the army withdrew, to board the last train with commissary items and protect them from the enemy. We worked hard all night, got everything aboard the train and saw it leave about daylight. So well did General Johns[t]on manage his retreat that not a handful of meal or any other commissary supplies were left behind. About sunrise, we took up our line of march for Resaca, about twenty miles away, where our army had gone during the night. A portion of General Sherman's army was following in our rear and came into Dalton on one side as we were going out on the other. They did not overtake us however and we made the march without being molested. When we reached Resaca, we found our men entrenched in hastily constructed earthworks and the enemy preparing for an attack.[46] As we had no sleep the night before and had made a long and tiresome march, we were not put in line but were allowed to rest and sleep. There was heavy firing all the afternoon. After dark, five companies of our regiment were assigned to a position in the rear of a battery on the incline of a steep hill. General Cheatham, when placing us here, said to us: "Boys, you must get deep down into the ground tonight. You are going to have a hot time tomorrow". We had only one pick and one shovel to make our entrenchment in a hard and gravely soil. We worked hard all night in relays—part of the men working while the others slept and by daylight the next morning, we had a trench about three feet deep and an embankment of earth thrown out of the trench in our front. These works were in plain view of the enemy's line on a ridge opposite to us, across an interweaving valley. Their line was concealed from our view by a growth of small timber.

Soon after daylight the next morning, a furious cannonade was opened upon our works by the enemy's battery not more than half

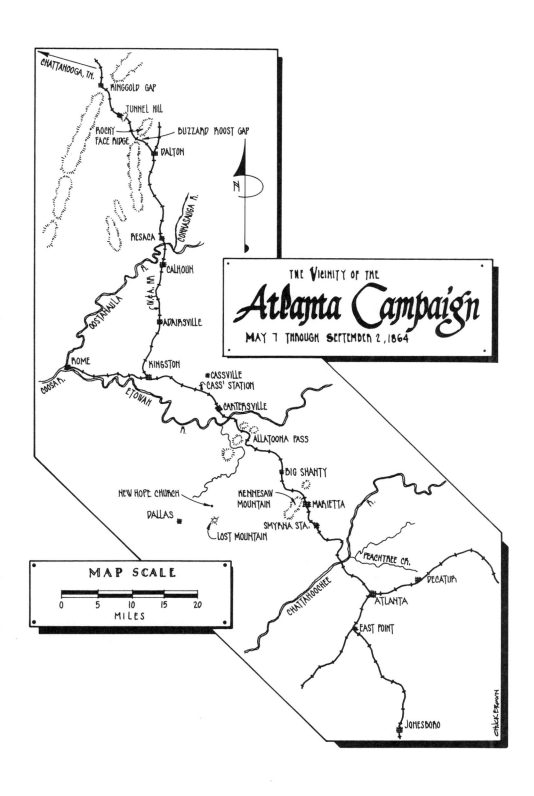

CHATTANOOGA, TN.

RINGGOLD GAP

TUNNEL HILL

ROCKY FACE RIDGE — BUZZARD ROOST GAP

DALTON

N

CONNASAUGA R.

RESACA

CALHOUN

OOSTANAULA

RIVER, M.

ADAIRSVILLE

ROME

KINGSTON

COOSA R.

ETOWAH

R.

CASSVILLE
CASS' STATION

CARTERSVILLE

ALLATOONA PASS

BIG SHANTY

NEW HOPE CHURCH

KENNESAW MOUNTAIN

MARIETTA

DALLAS

SMYRNA STA.

LOST MOUNTAIN

R.

PEACHTREE CR.

DECATUR

CHATTAHOOCHEE

ATLANTA

EAST POINT

JONESBORO

CHUCK BROWN

THE VICINITY OF THE

Atlanta Campaign

MAY 7 THROUGH SEPTEMBER 2, 1864

MAP SCALE

0   5   10   15   20
MILES

a mile away. They soon got our range and rarely missed their mark. Shell after shell exploded in the little bank of protecting earth, behind which we lay. And although this was kept up with occasional intervals during the entire day, the greater part of our embankment had been knocked in on us. By a merciful Providence, not one of our company was hurt. Not a man had been able to leave the trenches or even to raise his head or any portion of his body above our breastworks during the day, since our route of exit lay directly up the hill and would not only expose us to the fire of the battery, but also to that of the enemy's sharpshooters who were within easy range of us and from their concealed position, were keeping a steady watch on us. When night came, we crawled out of the dirt which had been tumbled in on us and were thankful that after such a dreadful experience, we were all alive. Our trench had been almost filled by the falling dirt. As we had been held in reserve, awaiting the attack of the enemy on the battery in our front, not a shot had been fired by our regiment during the day. A little after dark, when the fire of the enemy had ceased, General Cheatham came along our lines and said to us: "Boys, you'll have to stay here another day. You'd better get down in the ground as deep as you can". This was Saturday night. As I have said before, we had only one pick and one shovel to each company. We knew from the dreadful experience of the past day what we might certainly expect for the next. After a full discussion of the matter by the members of the company, it was unanimously decided, that as we had been protected by an overruling Providence during the past day and could only hope for that protection in the future as long as we lived in obedience to His law, to work with all our might at our trench until midnight and then to lie down and sleep until morning. Captain Rice[47] of the company next on our left, [upon] hearing the discussion, said to us: "If you men have any conscientious scruples about working on Sunday in such a place as this, I wish you would lend us your shovel and pick when you quit work at midnight". This we readily agreed to do. We began our work first by throwing out the loose earth that had been knocked in on us during the day and then sinking our trench as deep as we could in the limited time allowed for work. In addition to the fortification of the day before, we secured a stout head-log and put it in position on the top of our embankment. When midnight came, we handed our tools over to the next company, lay down in the trench and slept soundly until morning. The other companies had worked all night their trenches had been sunk much lower in the earth than ours. Soon after daylight the next morning, the enemy's batteries opened on us again and continued throughout the day to pour on us even a heavier fire of shot and shell than on the day before. Their sharpshooters were also on the watch and poured in a volley on whatever had an appearance of a man. I remember that one of our boys had left his knapsack, in which was rolled up a large new shawl which he had gotten from home, lying on the bank at the back of our trench and within reach if he had dared to put out his arm to get it. When we came out after night, he found the knapsack and blanket so completely riddled with bullets that he threw both away. There was not a piece of the shawl left as large as a man's hand.

The enemy's gunners, after keeping up their fire for about an hour, would be compelled to cease their fire for an hour or more to let their guns cool. This gave us several intervals of rest during the day. One of these, we improved by holding our regular Sunday evening Bible reading and prayer meeting. Some of the boys said afterward, that they did not remember very well what they read that evening. This reading was interrupted by a renewal of the enemy's fire. One of their balls striking our head-log, squarely cutting it in two and rolling it down on the men. We were all pretty badly scared but no one was seriously hurt. During this day, the firing was as continuous and as well directed as on the day before and our breastwork was battered down almost to the ground and yet not one of our men was hurt. About the middle of the afternoon, while the firing was at it's heaviest, we heard an outcry in Captain Rice's works close to us on our left. On calling to them to know what was the matter, Captain Rice called to us that he had two men killed and one wounded. A solid ball had forced its way through the earth in his front and passed through the men lying on the bottom of his trench. If they had quit work at midnight when we did, their trench would have been two feet shallower than it was and this ball would have made its way two feet under them. From midnight until daylight the next morning, these men had been digging their own graves. I have always regarded this as a wonderful Providence.

We were not able to leave our trenches until after dark when the firing ceased in our front. After coming out, we were marched down to Resaca where we found a large body of our troops awaiting the construction of a pontoon bridge across the Oostauaula river.[48] In our rear, General Sherman made a flank move, went to our left and this forced General Johnston to take a new position. The crossing was effected during the night in an orderly manner and without loss to our army.

Our next stand was made at Adairsville[49] where we had a sharp engagement with the enemy. In this battle, my brother, John's life, was saved by his Bible which he carried in the breast pocket of his coat. A minie ball passed almost through the book and but for this obstruction, would have gone through his body in the region of his heart. [With] General Sherman still continuing his flank movements, General Johnston was forced to abandon this place and afterwards, Kingston and Cass Station in succession. At Cartersville we had determined to make a stand but some of his corps commanders, being doubtful of their ability to maintain their positions against the greatly superior force of the enemy, he withdrew his troops across the Etowah River to a very strong position on the Kennesaw Mountain.

Up to this time, there had been continuous skirmishing with the enemy and except when we were changing position in the night, we were all the while under their fire. The character of the country had been such that General Sherman had not been forced to make an assault on our lines as he could make a flank movement without going too far from his base of supplies, the railroads.

Here, General Sherman, after an unsuccessful attack on our lines, moved his army to our left some twenty miles, with the intention of getting in our rear and forcing General Johnston to abandon his position.

Our corps (Cheatham's) was sent out to check his advance and was successful in doing this after a sharp engagement near Dallas on the 27th of May.[50] In this fight, I received a wound in the head from a small fragment of a shell which exploded very near me. Although the wound was slight, I was stunned by it and disabled for camp duty, Robert Lemmon was very severely, and as it afterwards proved, mortally wounded in this fight. Willie Holmes and John Sweet were also slightly wounded and went with me in a wagon down to Marietta and from there to the hospital at Macon, Georgia.

On our way down to Marietta, night came on us before we had made more than half the distance. We camped near a farm house in the neighborhood of Lost Mountain. As there was an appearance of rain, one of the boys went over and asked permission of the good man of the house for us to sleep on his front gallery. This request was kindly granted. When we went over, the old gentleman very kindly insisted on our coming into his house and occupying his best spare room. On glancing around the room after entering, I noticed a set of Scotts' Commentary in the book case and several copies of the "South Carolina Presbyterian" by me on the table. At the same time, the odor of the Saturday night loaf baking in the next room greeted my nostrils. I knew at once in what sort of a place our lives had fallen. I remarked to John Sweet, who had been brought up a Methodist and who by the way was one of the most conscientious and lovely boys that I have ever known, "These folks are going to have light bread for supper and are going to invite us out to eat with them". Sure enough in a little while, the old gentleman came in and invited us out to supper. To John's indent astonishment, there was a great loaf of light bread on the table. No one who has not undergone the hardships and poor scant fare can appreciate our enjoyment of that meal. After supper, John called me out and wanted to know of me, how I knew that we would be invited out to supper and if we would have warm light bread. I told him that these people were Presbyterians and that there was a sort of Free Masonry among all Presbyterians—that they had certain signs nobody else knew anything about. I shall never forget the kindness of these good people. They were living in daily expectation of Johnston's falling back and leaving them to the mercy of Sherman's vermins. Still, they seemed more solicitous for the comfort of we wounded soldiers than for their own fate. Of course, when our army withdrew, they would lose everything. I am sorry to say, we did not always find the natives of the country of like spirit.

I remember one day, when we were in the rear and the enemy following close behind us. We halted for a little while at a farm house where the people had a great abundance of poultry of all kinds. Our boys tried to buy some chickens from them and after haggling a long time, the owner agreed to take a dollar for one chicken. The boys gave chase and finally caught one. When they offered to pay the price asked for it, the owner objected, that was a very large chicken and he could not afford to take a dollar for it. Just then we were ordered to resume our march and came away without the chicken. The enemy were not more than ten minutes behind us and we knew and he ought to have known that Sherman's men were not in the habit of paying for their chickens.

After our delightful entertainment of Saturday night, we resumed our trip in the wagon and on reaching Marietta, took the train for Atlanta. Here, Willie Holmes and John Sweet remained over in the hospital while I was sent to Macon. On arriving there, I found my friend, Dr. Sol. Green in charge of one of the wards of the hospital. He very kindly provided for me the best accommodations his ward afforded. After I had been there several days, Mrs. Witherspoon, a refugee from Memphis whose sons had attended my school, came into the hospital and on learning that I was there, kindly invited me to her house. Here, I was most cordially received and for the remainder of my sick leave, enjoyed to the full, the hospitality of Mr. and Mrs. Witherspoon and their estimable family.

After being away about two weeks, being entirely recovered from my wound, I returned to the army. On my way back, I stopped over a day in Atlanta and went out to see our wounded in the hospital.

[I] found all doing well except Robert Lemmon, who was in a very critical condition, suffering from a gun shot wound through the liver. He did not live more than a day or two after I saw him. He was buried at the hospital graveyard and after the war was over, his body was disinterred and bought back to the old Mountain graveyard where it now lies.[51]

During my absence, our army had retired to a strong position on the Kennesaw line. Our corps was stationed near the extreme left of our line. I remember that I had difficulty in finding my company. We kept this line with occasional changes of position without coming to a general engagement with the enemy, although there was heavy skirmishing going on both day and night during the whole time—until the 27th of June.[52] On this day, General Sherman assaulted our lines with a heavy force in several places. The most furious assault was made on that part of the line which happened to be occupied by our brigade (Maney's). The nature of the ground in our front was such as to give the enemy the opportunity of forming their line of battle within a hundred yards of our works—entirely out of our sight. Here, General Sherman had concentrated a whole corps and had formed them in five lines, one immediately behind the other. We were not expecting the attack and the part of the works held by Colonel Field's regiment of our brigade (First Tennessee) immediately on our right, was inefficiently manned, from the fact that Colonel Field, not expecting an attack, had allowed a number of his men to go [to] the rear of the breastworks during the heat of the engagement. So that we had the double duty of keeping off the enemy and changing our position at the same time. It was an extremely hot day and the fight lasted from 11 o'clock A.M. until noon. The ground in front of us was literally blue with Yankees. Their advance column reached our breastworks and planted their flag on them, but the resistance of our men was so determined that they did not dare to come over. Only the breastworks divided the two armies. We had the advantage of having a head-log on our side of the works and the enemy were crowded so thickly that a shot from our men could not fail to hit somebody.

I remember that when I was trying to push my company as rapidly as possible to the right, I noticed one man, Jim Goforth, who had just finished loading his gun, suddenly halt and raise his gun to his shoulder thereby obstructing our movement to the right. I called to him to move forward. His reply was: "Just wait Captain, till I kill this Yankee". He immediately fired across the breastworks and turning to me with "I got him", resumed his march.

To show how hot the place was and how incessant the firing, one of my men brought his gun to me, choked and rendered useless by melted lead. The thin shaving of lead pared off from the minie ball by the grooves of our rifles when melted, ran down into the tubes of the guns when held in an upright position. To prevent this, I ordered the men to reverse their guns after firing so that the lead might run out at the muzzle. When they did this, I saw small round pellets of melted lead poured out of their gun barrels on the ground. After the fight had gone on this way for some time, a terrific cannonade of shell and grape was opened upon the three rear columns of the enemy from one of our batteries stationed on our left in such a position that their fire enfiladed the enemy lines. All this was more than they could stand. After a fierce assault on our lines, which lasted about an hour, they gave up the attack and retired to their sheltered position under the hill in our front. I remember that when I looked at my watch after the battle was over and found that we had been fighting an hour, I was greatly surprised at the length of time. We had been kept so busy that the time seemed shorter. I have mentioned that the Yankees had planted their colors on our works. Notwithstanding a desperate effort on the part of our men to capture these in which three men lost their lives, they were carried away safely by the retreating enemy, but at a great cost of life to them.

After the enemy had retired and we could survey the ground in our front which they had just occupied, a frightful and disgusting scene of death and destruction was presented to our view. During all of the four years of the war, I do not remember ever to have seen the ground so completely strewn with dead bodies. The loss on our part was very small, only two or three wounded in the regiment— not one in my company. As I have said above, the enemy, after their repulse, withdrew to a position under the hill out of our view. Here, they threw up breastworks within fifty yards of our lines. The two armies occupied this position for several days, both strongly entrenched behind breastworks and near enough to be in plain view of each other when anyone was imprudent enough to raise his head above the works. A continued fire of small arms was kept up all the while both day and night between the two lines. The enemy were so near that we were in constant fear of a renewal of their attack.

The nights were very dark but we were supplied with turpentine balls which we threw lighted over our works into the space between the two lines whenever we heard any suspicious noise in our front. After a continuous watch of more than thirty six hours without rest or sleep, we were relieved some time during the second night after the battle by another regiment. I remember that when I got my company out of the trenches, I got permission of the commanding officer to go three miles back in the rear to our wagon train, clear away from the din of battle and get a good night's sleep. In this, however, I was somewhat disappointed, for soon after I had lain down and before I was soundly asleep, I was aroused by one of the most terrific volleys of musketry that I ever heard which was kept up continuously for half an hour. As this was in the direction of the point we had just left, I very naturally concluded that the enemy had made the attack upon our works which we had been so long expecting and that a fierce battle was in progress. After a while, the firing ceased and all was quiet and I slept undisturbed until morning. I have to this day a grateful recollection of the hot corn dodger and the fried middling served up to me the next morning by my good friend, Joe Forsythe.

When I got back to my regiment, I learned that there had been no battle, but that the men who had taken our place in the works, becoming alarmed at some unusual sound or appearance in their front, had opened the firing and that it was returned by the enemy from their breastworks.

After a day's rest, we returned to our former position in the works, I recall toward one or two incidents of our stay here which may be interesting to my children. One was that late in the first night after the battle, while we were on watch in the trenches, I was sitting on a bank of earth with my head leaning against an upright post driven in the ground to steady the head-log. I was so worn out with fatigue and loss of sleep that notwithstanding the fact that a brisk skirmish fire was going on all the while, I fell asleep. In my sleep, I dreamed that I was back at home once more and that I was sitting with my little girls—one on each knee. While in this position a wardrobe or some heavy piece of furniture seemed to fall to the floor with a crash, jarring the whole house. This noise of course, awakened me and I found that the crash was caused by a bullet striking the post against which I was leaning, a few inches above my head. This was a rude awakening from such a pleasant dream.

Another incident was a sad one. When we were relieved on the second night, Colonel Jones, commander of the relieving troops, came into the works just where I was stationed. I pointed out to him the seat I had been occupying during the day and recommended it as a comfortable seat and a safe place. We had not been out of the works twenty minutes before he was killed in the very place I had just left—a glancing ball deflected from its course by the lower side of the head-log and passed through his head. If we had been relieved twenty minutes later, I should have been killed instead of him.

LEGEND
☐ C.S. TROOPS
■ U.S. TROOPS
⊨ ARTILLERY
~~~~ INTRENCHMENTS

D A V I S

N E W T O N

MITCHELL   McCOOK   HARKER   WAGNER   KIMBALL

G E A R Y

CANDY
IRELAND
JONES

NOSE'S

CREEK

LOWERY
POLK   CLEBURNE

V A U G H A N

1/27 TH
19 TH
4/50 TH
6/9 TH

M A N E Y

THE DEAD ANGLE

N

C H E A T H A M

MAP SCALE

0   1000   2000
FEET

CARTER

THE
NINTH TENNESSEE INFANTRY
(MANEY'S BRIGADE)
Dead Angle
KENNESAW MOUNTAIN, GEORGIA
JUNE 27, 1864

We remained in this position, in all, a week or ten days. During all this time, skirmish firing between the two lines never ceased day or night. The enemy had fared so badly in their first assault on our works that they did not afterwards repeat the attack. Sherman finally resorted to his usual expedient—a flank movement to our left. This compelled the withdrawal of our troops from this position. We were withdrawn in the night so quietly and with so little confusion that the enemy immediately in our front did not seem to be aware of this movement. Our next position was in the neighborhood of Atlanta, across the Chattahoochee river. General Johnston, expecting to be forced to fall back to this point, had strengthened a position naturally strong by the erection of earthworks. His plan was to make a final stand here. For a few days, we had rest. The enemy were slow in crossing the river and in making their preparations for attack. The campaign thus far had been managed with consummate skill by General Johnston. Our losses both of men and material had been trifling. For nearly three months, we had presented a bold front to the enemy and never gave way except when compelled to do so by a flank movement on their part which, on account of their great superiority in numbers, they had no trouble in making. In fact, they could keep a force equal to ours in front, and at the same time, send an equal or superior force around on our flank. Every assault made on our works had been repulsed—some of them notably—at New Hope Church and Kennesaw Mountain, with terrible slaughter. Our army was in good health and in good spirits. Our rations—cold corn dodger, two or three days old and raw bacon with an occasional ration of dry cow peas, which we cooked in tin cans, were abundant and filling. After we crossed the Chattahoochee, General Johnston ordered the army to be supplied with a ration of vegetables. My company drew two beets and half dozen potatoes. I happened to learn why these rations were so scant. Having gotten a leave of absence for one day, I went into Atlanta to get some things that I needed. On my way there, I spent the night at a Quartermaster's camp. There, I found a profusion of vegetables and nice things to eat intended for the men at the front which were being monopolized by [the] quartermaster's commissaries and their camp followers. I noticed on the supper table that night, a larger quantity of vegetables than were furnished to our whole regiment.

Very soon after we had occupied the works around Atlanta, we were amazed and distressed by the removal of General Johnston from the command of our army. President Davis, dissatisfied with Johnston's policy, removed him from command and appointed General Hood in his place. In the judgment of Johnston's army, it was the worst thing that could have been done. Up to this time, General Johnston was the only commander we had ever had, in whose ability and generalship the army had unlimited confidence. I do not remember that I ever heard any order or movement of General Johnston's, infavorably criticized by his men. I can not say so much for General Bragg. General Hood had proved himself a gallant soldier and an efficient corps commander not only in the Virginia army but also in our army. He was a good fighter but inclined to be rash and up to this time had never been entrusted with a separate command. His conduct of the campaign, after taking command, showed him to be utterly incompetent to discharge the duties of commander in chief. The removal of Johnston and appointment of Hood was more demoralizing to our army than the loss of a great battle would have been. No better evidence of their patriotism and devotion to duty could have been shown than their prompt obedience to orders and heroic bravery even when they knew that their general was incompetent and that they were being foolishly sacrificed. Johnston, by his skillful generalship, had compelled the enemy to attack him in his breastworks. Hood foolishly undertook to drive a force greatly superior to his own out of their works with the result that our loss was fearful. Three times our men were ordered to attack the enemy in their works—first on the 20th of July on Peach Tree Creek.[53] Here our brigade formed the supporting line and though under fire, was not brought into action. The position of the enemy was so strong and the loss of our front line so heavy that the attack was abandoned without bring up the reserves. From where we lay in reserve, we had a plain view of the battle in our front and though not actually engaged, suffered considerable loss from the enemy's fire.

I call to mind a remarkable Providence to my company here. While we were lying on the ground in the rear line, a cannonball from the enemy's batteries struck a pine tree under which we were lying, cutting the trunk almost in two about half-way up the tree. The top fell but was held by some splinters which prevented its falling to the ground. Being afraid that it would fall on us, I moved my company back twenty paces to the rear of the line where we again lay down. Immediately after this movement was made, a large shell struck the ground directly on the spot where we had been lying a minute before and exploded with terrific force, scattering earth and fragments of the shell in every direction. The warning given by the broken tree top had saved the lives of many if not all the company. The loss of our army in this attack was very heavy and nothing was accomplished.

Two days afterward, on July 22nd, occurred the bloody and disastrous battle of Decatur.[54] General McClernand's corps had fortified a very strong position here on the extreme left of the Federal line. The object of the attack was to drive the enemy from their position. We left our temporary camp, about three miles east of Atlanta, about daylight and marched by a circuitous route—first south some four or five miles from Atlanta, then east over country roads about the same distance, then again moved to the point of attack. We did not reach this place until the afternoon. General Hood had expected to find them unprotected by fortifications in this direction. In this he was disappointed. We found the enemy strongly entrenched in a double line of breastworks about four hundred yards apart. Our division was first moved to the extreme right of our line where it was intended that we should make an attack, however, after marching in line of battle for more than a mile through a dense undergrowth of bushes and brambles, we were stopped by an impassable creek and millpond before we reached our point of attack. Finding it impossible to go any farther, we were withdrawn and double quicked to the extreme left. The day was excessively hot and our marching and counter-marching had greatly wearied us. Here we found that General Cleburne's division had captured the first line of the enemy's works while we had been delayed in our ineffectual movement on the right. It was now about five o'clock in the evening when we passed over the line of works captured by Cleburne and formed in line of battle immediately in the rear of them. The second line was about four hundred yards in front of us on top of a ridge. In the space between the two lines of works was an old field on which no crop was growing but the deep furrows and ridges showed plainly that it had been cultivated last in corn. There were a few old trees and stumps scattered about in this space. One man seemingly dead lay within a very short distance in front of our company. As soon as I had completed the alignment of my company, I walked forward a few steps [to] where this man was lying. I discovered that although he had a horrible wound in the neck, he was still breathing. He had been lying there for hours in the blistering sunshine and his lips were parched and dry. I huddled down beside him, unstopped my canteen and poured some water down his throat. I can never forget his look of gratitude when he opened his eyes and fixed them on me with the exclamation: "Bully for you". A little in advance of us was one of Cleburne's men kneeling behind a stump with his gun pointed toward the enemy and seemingly in the act of firing. As we passed him in our advance, I noticed that he was dead—had been killed instantly by a ball which struck him in the forehead. This was one of the rare instances in which I have observed that a man kept the same position after death that he had taken while living.

Before we had completed our alignment and begun our advance, a fierce discharge of small arms and artillery was opened on our line from the works in our front. Even before we had begun the advance, many of our men were shot down and as we approached nearer to their works, their fire became still more deadly. As I looked down the line, I could see men dropping by the scores. When we had gone about half the distance on glancing to the right, I saw Junius Hall, who commanded a company immediately on my right, fall to the ground. I ran across to where he lay and saw that he was dead—killed instantly by a bullet through his heart. His face was lovely in death as it had been in life. There was no trace of pain in his face which beamed with the same happy smile that he wore in life. A moment afterwards, I was struck by a rifle ball in my right thigh which disabled me so much that I could go no farther. As I turned to make my way to the rear, another bullet passed through my left thigh. I was so stunned by the second shot that I fell to the ground. I happened to fall in the furrow between two of the old corn ridges that I mentioned above. As I fell, the stopper came out of my canteen but I had sufficient presence of mind to search around

The bullet-riddled Dalton issue "Battle Flag" of the 6th & 9th consolidated Tennessee Infantry Regiment.

until I found it, thus saving the water which I so much needed and which was so grateful to me during the three or four hours that I lay here.

Our troops succeeded in capturing the second line of works for a short distance (a few hundred yards) but for want of support, were compelled to retire after nightfall. Here General McClernand was killed. I lay in the place where I had fallen until after dark. During all this time, the ground on which I lay was swept by a terrific hail of bullets and cannon shot fired from that part of the enemy's line on our right which we had failed to capture. Providentially, I had fallen in a protected spot and the bullets whistled two or three feet above me.

I remember that the crash of bullets against an old tree which stood near me was as continuous as the ringing of a bell. I did not suffer any great pain from my wound but was weakened by the loss of blood. When it began to grow dark and the firing in a measure ceased, one of our infirmary corps, Jerry Farrel, a stalwart Irishman, came in where I was lying and told me that he had been waiting for two hours for an opportunity to carry me out and although the firing had not entirely ceased, he had at last concluded to risk it. He took me on his shoulder and started out with me but discovering that I had fainted, laid me down again with the promise that he would return with a stretcher as soon as he could get some of the other boys to come with him. In about half an hour, when it had become quite dark and the firing had ceased, he came in with two other men and carried me back to the field hospital. The surgeons, on examination, pronounced one of my wounds, (the one in my left thigh) probably mortal. The ball had passed so near the femoral artery that in case of any sloughing[55] of the wound, amputation of the leg would be necessary. This however would be impossible on account of the nearness of the wound to the hip joint. I felt encouraged however, by my experience with the wound received at Perryville and was not afraid of sloughing.

From the beginning of the war, I had made it my invariable practice to carry with me in my knapsack, a good supply of lint, bandages and castile soap. And as I was fortunate enough always to have an attendant of my own choosing, I never let a hospital nurse put his hands on me. In this way, I avoided entirely gangrene of the wound—that terrible pest of hospitals. While I was lying on the field, a young man by the name of Thomas, belonging to our regiment, lay wounded about a rod from me. Late in the evening, he asked me how I was wounded and when told that I was shot in both legs, asked if my legs were broken. I told him that I hoped not, that I could work my feet and toes and that I considered this a good

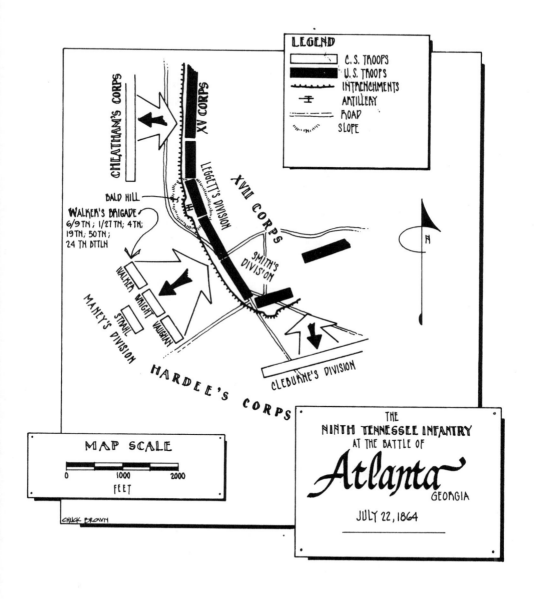

LEGEND

▭	C.S. TROOPS
▬	U.S. TROOPS
⊥⊥⊥⊥⊥	INTRENCHMENTS
⊣Ⓔ⊢	ARTILLERY
— — —	ROAD
⏜⏜⏜	SLOPE

CHEATHAM'S CORPS

XV CORPS

LEGGETT'S DIVISION

XVII CORPS

BALD HILL

WALKER'S BRIGADE
6/9 TN; 1/27 TN; 4TH;
19TH; 50TH;
24TH BTTLN

SMITH'S DIVISION

WALKER

WRIGHT

STRAHL

VAUGHAN

MANEY'S DIVISION

HARDEE'S CORPS

CLEBURNE'S DIVISION

N

MAP SCALE

0   1000   2000
FEET

THE
NINTH TENNESSEE INFANTRY
AT THE BATTLE OF
Atlanta
GEORGIA

JULY 22, 1864

CHUCK BROWN

sign. He replied: "If that's any sign, I am all right, see how I can work my leg". With that he turned on his back, raised his leg and worked it back and forth several times without any pain. He was shot through the knee. The next morning at the field hospital, when I inquired of the surgeon how Thomas was getting along, he told me that he had died in the night. When I told the surgeon what had passed between us the evening before, he said that the absence of pain in his wound was the worst possible sign—that ordinarily a wound in the knee was the most painful of all wounds and that his freedom from pain was an evidence of the complete prostration of his nervous system. We remained at this temporary hospital until 9 o'clock A.M. when the reopening of the enemy's fire rendered it unsafe for us to remain there any longer.

I remember an amusing incident that occurred at this place in which my benefactor, Jerry Farrel, was the actor. Some of our men had brought away with them from the enemy's works, some hard-tack and as this was a rarity, it was left for the wounded. Friend Jerry, in passing along, picked up one of the crackers and striking an attitude said: "Boys, I haven't seen a cracker in a long time and I am going to eat this one". When he had gotten it within about six inches of his mouth, a bullet struck it in the center, scattering all of it in every direction except the little corner he held between his thumb and finger. With a puzzled look on his face, he hesitated a moment, then put the little fragment that was left in his mouth saying, "I will get this much of it anyway". Poor old Jerry was killed at Franklin, Tennessee not long afterward.

On the 23rd, we were moved some five miles to the rear to our field hospital near Cobbs' Mill. Here, I stayed until the next day. Our wounded and dead were all brought to this place. Here I succeeded in getting a coffin made of rough boards for Junius Hall and saw him placed in it. His body remained here until the next year when it was removed and reinterred in the Mountain graveyard at home. On the 24th, my thirty-seventh birthday, I was put with other wounded men on the floor of a box car to be conveyed to the hospital at Macon, Georgia. Joseph Hall, who had been slightly wounded, went with me and I recall to mind with gratitude, his untiring kindness on the train and at the hospital. On our way, the train stopped at Griffin. James Peter Holmes was here in charge of our medical stores. When he saw my uncomfortable position, lying with nothing between me and the bare floor except my blanket, he ran to a fodder stack nearby and appropriated fodder enough to make me a comfortable bed.

When our train reached Milner's Station where we had a hospital for the wounded, thinking that I was too much exhausted by the trip to go any farther, the surgeon in charge of the train ordered me to be put off here. This was the best regulated hospital that I was ever in. It was under the control of Dr. Westmoreland of Atlanta, a man eminently fitted for hospital work.[56] The hospital accommodations consisted of large tents, capable of holding ten men each, furnished with comfortable cots. These tents were pitched in a beautiful grove of pines where we had plenty of pure air. The weather was very warm and we were far better off here than if we had been shut up in close houses. The fare was good or abundant. For the sick, it was wheat bread and chicken with it['s] accompaniments in small quantities. For the convalescent, bacon and greens, cornbread in abundance. I was fortunate enough to be placed on the sick list with a convalescent appetite. To make up the deficiency in quantity, Joseph Hall found a good lady in the neighborhood who furnished me with a nice smothered chicken and a dozen well baked biscuits three times a week. With this supply, in addition to my hospital rations, I managed to get along comfortably.

The surgeon in charge of the ward in which I was placed, on examining my wounds, looked very grave and remarked to me: "My friend, you have a very bad wound and I am afraid that you will be in for a long time if you ever get out alive". I assured him: "If you will let me have my way, I will be on my legs in a month". I told him that I had everything necessary for dressing my wounds and if he would furnish me a wash pan, I would not need the services of the hospital nurses. He agreed to this. While Joseph stayed with me, he dressed my wounds and after he left at the end of a week, the surgeon himself was kind enough to do it for me. As a diversion while lying here on my back, I read almost the whole of Virgil's Aeneid from a small Leipzig edition which, with my Bible, I carried with me throughout the war in my knapsack. While I was here, my brother John, visited me. He had been very severely injured a month or more before this, while our army was on the Kennesaw line. One evening about dark while he, with several others, was lying on the ground resting, a tree fell on the party, which besides doing serious injury to several others, dislocated his hip. I had been sent for immediately after the occurrence and had gone to him several miles away after night. He was nearly five miles from the field hospital. The roads were almost impassable and the night was very dark. He was carried this long distance through mud almost knee deep on a litter, by men from his regiment. It took five hours to travel the distance and we arrived at the hospital after daylight. Dr. Roane, who was in charge of the hospital, administered chloroform and got the joint back in position. This injury disabled him for service for several months and lamed him for life. I think that he was on

Captain James Iredell Hall
July 24, 1827–January 29, 1910

Born in Iredell County, North Carolina, he and his
family moved first to Hardeman County, Tennessee,
then to Tipton County in 1834. An 1847 graduate of
Centre College, Danville, Kentucky, Captain Hall
returned home to teach. He assisted in the
organization of Company C, 9th Tennessee Infantry
and was seriously wounded at Perryville,
Chickamauga and Atlanta. He was first married to
Miss Sarah Lemmon and in 1866 was married to Miss
Mary Hall. He is buried in the Mt. Carmel Cemetery,
Tipton County, Tennessee.

his way home when he visited me as I do not remember seeing him afterwards until I got home. I remained at this hospital two weeks before I could get the consent of the surgeon to go down to Macon. I had been so kindly treated by Mrs. Witherspoon some time before, that I was anxious to get back to her house. On my arrival at Macon, I was carried in an ambulance to the hospital. Here my friend, Dr. Green, ordered me to be driven directly to Mrs. Witherspoon's. Junius Hall's servant, Bill, was with me and remained with me as long as I needed his services.

Captain Hall's Daughter's Epilogue

Papa was home until the Spring of 1865 when he started back to the army. He was taken sick at Warrenton, Georgia so [he] failed to reach Greensboro in time for the surrender. He made his way home by slow stages.

Mount Carmel Presbyterian Church
Located approximately 5 miles southwest of Covington, Tennessee.
This is the central structure of the Mt. Carmel community and was
built in the late 1850s. It is on the National Register of Historic Places
and is one of the few buildings of the ante-bellum period that remain
standing in Mount Carmel.

Since his name did not appear in the list of soldiers surrendered, I asked Papa the cause and his answer was: "Because I was mortally wounded at Perryville". He had been pronounced dead and according to army regulations, could not be restored to life, although wounded twice after that.

END

Captain James Iredell Hall was born on July 24, 1827, and died on January 29, 1910. During his 82 years, he amassed a fortune few men even dream of. Though not necessarily a monetary fortune, he attained the love and affection afforded only those few who not only educate a generation but guide and lead those students into, and out of, the depth of war's fierce cauldrons. He pledged the parents of his students to remain with and watch over them throughout their military service, which he did, while exuding the chivalrous and honorable character reminiscent of a royal knight. He performed his duties with a conviction only equaled by his religious convictions. As his obituary states: "his comrades with one voice proclaim his as one of the most gallant and intrepid who wore the gray."

After the fall of the Confederacy, Captain Hall returned to Mount Carmel to resume his previous vocation of educator and re-opened the Mountain Academy. He once again became a pillar of the community and served the Mount Carmel Presbyterian Church for the balance of his life.

These reminiscences were probably written shortly after the May, 1895 dedication of the monument to Tipton County's Confederate Veterans and were prompted by Captain C. B. Simonton's articles. It appears to have been written solely for the education and enjoyment of his children. We, as children of another generation, will now be permitted to glean and enjoy these memoirs as his children did nearly a century ago.

CHAPTER 4

Chapters 4, 5, 6, and 7 contain letters that exemplify the reaction of four different personalities under the stress associated with conflict: a captain, sergeant, corporal, and a private soldier. Though their duties and responsibilities differ, sometimes greatly, their interests, attitudes and even levels of education appear strangely similar. They were all fairly close neighbors, devoutly Presbyterian and together, they experienced horrors and pain few others could imagine. All four soldiers were wounded at least once. Two of them were to die in battle.

Captain Hall's letters (Chapter 4) were preserved by his family and now reside in the Southern Historical Collection at the University of North Carolina at Chapel Hill. Typed copies of the McCreight and McDill letters (Chapters 5, 6, and 7) were found lying on the floor in the attic of my grandma's home after her death. Along with these heirlooms, I discovered a note written by George W. McDill (Chapter 7) which listed the battles in which he participated and the names of the survivors of the company at the close of the war.

Details in these letters are sometimes sketchy and sometimes pronounced. Those letters have not been stylistically nor punctually altered so that their full impact will reach the modern reader without interference from modern sources.

WARTIME CORRESPONDENCE OF
CAPTAIN JAMES IREDELL HALL

Captain James I. Hall was a family man. In most, if not all of his letters, he mentions his children. His early letters exhibit a naiveté concerning the rigors of hard campaigning. But toward the end of his service, his letters began to exhibit doubt and exhaustion. He no longer attempted to "put on a face," even for his children.

The Atlanta Campaign letters were the last to be saved by his family. Wounded in action near Decatur, Georgia during the Battle

85

of Atlanta, Hall was once again declared mortally wounded but through his own ingenuity, recovered, in order to miraculously journey to his home in West Tennessee. He recuperated there, until the spring of 1865 when he attempted to rejoin his former general, Joseph E. Johnston, in North Carolina. Falling ill at Warrenton, Georgia, he failed to reach Greensboro in time for the surrender. From Warrenton, he returned home.

Jackson [Tennessee] May 28/[18]61

Mr. & Mrs. J.S. Hall

Dear Parents,

I take this opportunity to write you a few lines. I arrived here the next morning after leaving home & have been quite well since, [I] have not staid in camp at night, [I] have been treated with great kindness by friends here particularly by Dr. Jackson & Mrs. J. The boys from the neighborhood are all well and are conducting themselves well.

Our company has taken a high stand. Mr. [Captain David Josiah] Wood could be elected Colonel of the regiment almost without opposition, but will not leave his company. We will be formed into a regiment this evening, [I] do not know when we will leave for Union City, probably soon.

There was a rumor yesterday of a negro insurrection in the neighborhood, but it was entirely without foundation. Our fare here is plain, but abundant & good. Gabe makes a very good cook, [he] is in fine spirits & is doing well. Stephen Carnes, John Matthews & Robt. Bullock are here & will be in our regiment. I should like to see you all particularly the children, [I] don't know when I will be at home. I hope the children are well, [I] would like to see them. This will be taken to you by Charley Hill who is reporting [to] his company. I wish you to write to me soon. Kis[s] the children for me.

From your afft. son
Jas I. Hall

(Mr. & Mrs. J.D. Hall
Mountain, Tipton Co. Tenn.)

Union City, June 5th [1861]

Dear Parents,

When I wrote to you last we were at Jackson. Our company came here last Saturday. I remained in Jackson till Monday on business for the company. It was quite a treat to spend the sabbath in quiet. While in Jackson, I spent most of the time in camp   slept in the tents at night   have been doing the same since I came here. we are very comfortably fixed   have a good tent, good cotton mattress, chairs etc. We have provisions in abundance and of good quality. We were however glad to see the nice box of provisions [illegible] anything from home tastes good. There is some sickness in the camp. one or two cases of mumps, one case of pneumonia and some bowel complaints.

Dumpy Daniel has had a mild attack of flux. is now well, the three boys from the neighborhood are well. There are five Regiments here, composed of between 5 & 6 Thousand men. We are encamped within 1 mile of Union City & forty miles of a place Wilson Matthews lives near here. was in camp yesterday. We have received our guns—percussion muskets. since we came here and are drilling with them. Mr. Wood has written to cousin Mattie to come up. If Jessie had not gone back to school I would want cousin Mattie to bring her & sissy up with her.

I do not know when I will go home   probably not soon if my health remains good. I am now quite well. You need not send any more provisions for the present, as we are doing well enough. If you send anything, send light bread   I was glad to learn by Johns note that you are all well. My love to the children. I want them to come up soon. Mr. Wood wishes to be remembered to you

From your afft son
Jas I Hall

Union City, June 9th [1861]

Dear Parents

It is Sunday night. There is preaching in the camp to night but as I have heard two sermons today & feel tired I will write home instead of attending preaching   I have been quite well since I came here with the exception of one spell of headache. I think that camp life will agree with me. The boys from the neighborhood are all well   There is some sickness in the camp but not severe so far. We have had a quiet day   no drilling or work   have a delightful encampment in a shady grove. are rather scarce of water but are digging wells and will soon have plenty. have just finished the box of provisions you sent us. the corn bread spoiled   We get an abundance of good provisions. don't want any thing but light bread and butter. We shall expect some of you up soon   The camp is crowded with visitors from all parts of the district. We are making arrangements to have a tent made for the accommodation of our friends.

Some of the boys were up today to the Miss. troops about half a mile above us. saw Ed Stitt & Joe Ross who was in my school   Capt Wood Mr. Winford and myself occupying the same tent. have a pleasant time. Cousin Wilson M. came to the camp frequently. had his wife with him today   she is an agreeable woman   We hav[e] not done much yet in the way of drilling   have been busy preparing our grounds. do not know how long we will stay here. I would like to see you all. do not expect to go home soon   want the children to come up if we stay here long   Let me know when the examination takes place   My love to the children

Your Afft son

Jas I Hall

Misses Jesse & Mary E. Hall

c/o Doctor W. M. Hall

Covington

Tipton Co.

Camp Brown, June 11, 61

Dear Children

I expect that you would like to get a letter from your papa. I am at Union City camped out in the woods. Mr Wood, Mr Winford Gabe and I stay in the same tent. Sometimes I sleep with the Captain sometimes with Gabe. We have the ground covered with straw, sleep on a mattress, have plenty of blankets. Gabe cooks for us. We have fried ham, biscuit and coffee for breakfast, dinner and supper. sometimes we get peas, beans, onions and potatoes for dinner. Grandma sent us some nice butter but it is almost gone. We have plenty to eat   Gabe washes for us   There are six regiments here now & we expect two or three more to day. I do not know how long we will stay here. we may go to Columbus very soon   when we go there we will have a great deal of hard work to do.

I will not have to work much myself. Our camp here is close beside the railroad. a great many cars pass every day & night. the whistle wakes us up every night

4D   34

CAMP BEAUREGARD

Among the Confederate units activated and trained in the staging area which stood here were the 6th Tenn. Infantry (Stephens), 9th Tenn. Infantry (Douglass), 12th Tenn. Infantry (Russell), 13th Tenn. Infantry (Wright), and 15th Tenn. Infantry (Carroll). The camp was activated in May, 1861; Col. William H. Stephens, CSA. was its first commander. Normal procedure was for companies to organize in their home communities, then to repair here for organization into regiments.

TENNESSEE HISTORICAL COMMISSION

Tennessee Historical Marker of Camp Beauregard, currently the site of a service station in Jackson, Tennessee.

I would like to be at home for the concert. if Jessie will play her piece well, but I cant get away. If we stay here long, I want you both to come up to see me after the session is out. While I am writing, another regiment has come on a train of cars as long as from Grandpas house to the gin. The men are in box cars they have knocked all the planks off from the sides of the cars and are standing with their heads out at the openings, looking like chickens in a chicken wagon. That is the way our company came up from Jackson. We have a great deal of noise in the camp at night. some of the boys sing, some holler, some bark like dogs, some crow like chickens and one whistles so much like a mocking bird that you would think that it was a bird indeed at nine o clock the lights are blown out and all go to bed except the guards who walk around the camp all night. They have a hard time when it rains. We see ladies and little girls in the camp every day, who come in to see the soldiers. seeing little girls here, reminds me of my little girls at home. I wonder if they are well and doing well and wish that I could see them for a little while. I want Jessie to write to me write a letter with a pencil and get aunt Sarah to direct it. I can read it   Let sissy tell Jessie something to write. Let me know how you both do   how Grandma & Grandpa & all the family do. Give my love to all your uncles & aunts & Cousins

From your papa
Jas I Hall

Direct letters to the care of
Capt. Wood 5 Regmt. Tenn Vol
Union City

New Madrid Aug 18. [1861]

Dear Parents

As I have an opportunity of sending a letter to day I will write a few lines. As you are aware we have been here two weeks. I have been quite well since I left home Was a little fatigued by the march across from Union City. We are here in a state of suspense. One day we are ordered to advance and the next, the order is countermanded. Last Sunday we spent at Randolph. It was hard to be so near you   We did not land at Fulton, consequently did not see John

Co. Neely's Regiment has just landed. I am again disappointed in not seeing John. His Regt is going up the country. We will follow in a day or two. Three Regts have left.

We will send home all unnecessary baggage   We expect to go twenty miles up the country to a place called Saxton   dont know where from there probably on to st Louis. Will march by easy stages, Knapsacks carried in wagons. Health of our Regt good. Boys in good spirits

Came near having a fight last week. Three gunboats came in sight but did not attack us. Old Granny Polk concluded that the place was unhealthy and left in the midst of the alarm. He deserves to be presented with a petticoat.

I should like to see you all particularly the children. dont expect to go home soon. You can do as you think best about sending Jessie to school   Cant you let Henry come up to

see us. We will keep near the river on our march   My love
to the children. tell Jessie to write
                    Your afft son
                    Jas I Hall

[Mrs. R.M. Hall
Mountain, Tenn.]

                                    Columbus sept 19 [1861]

    Dear Parents
    You will be surprised to learn that we are again at this
place. We came up yesterday on the Rail Road after marching eight miles the night before. Col stevens' Regt was with
us. had a pleasant time down at fulton on the state
line   men kindly treated by the people. our boys are all
well and enjoying themselves hugely over the box of good
things sent up by John Calhoun, as it was the first we have
had since we left Union City. I was glad to hear when I got
here that John had gone home as he was not well. Things
here remain about as they were. Genl Cheatham with his
Brigade is coming in to day from Mayfield. Col Neely's Regt
has moved two miles up the river
    We have between twenty five and thirty thousand troops
here now   Genl Johnson is said to have arrived here last
night. I have not seen him but suppose that it is true. We
have been very anxious for his coming. have not had confidence in our leaders. think that Johnson is a man who can
be relied on
    I have been greatly gratified by letters from Ma, William,
sister Mary Eliza and Jessie   say to sister M.E. that I will
write to her soon. Doct Jackson is here tonight
    We are all glad to know that our friends at home are
preparing for our comfort during the next winter. We will
have to rely entirely upon the exertions of our friends for a
supply of winter clothing since the quartermasters stores
are exhausted. for myself I shall need nothing except a good
warm pair of pants, as I have a sufficiency of other clothing
at home. I shall try to get home in time to make preparation
for the winter. We will probably be actively employed for the
next two months and will not want any superfluous baggage. We must have our clothing though before the winter
sets in. Tell Jessie that I would like to have a pair of socks of
her knitting. Give my love to the children. I want very much

to see them. Spencer Hall is with us tonight   goes home in the morning. My love to all my friends

Your afft son
Jas I Hall

Columbus sept 25 [1861]

Dear Brother

Dr Ligon is here and will take this to you. We are still at Columbus. do not know how long we will stay. am clearing off a new camping ground about a mile from town on the bluff   expect to move in a day or two   am now camped in a low wet place

It rained the other night. camped diluged with water shoe mouth deep in the tents. I coiled up in [a] goods Box and slept soundly   We are now hard at work on the batteries. on fortifying the place strongly   dont expect to have to run from here. It is rumored that we will make an advance movement after the fortifications are completed. The enemy have a body of troops stationed about ten miles above us on the river. Our cavalry are sent up there every day to watch their movements. We do not fear an attack here. The Mississippi and Louisiana troops are leaving here for the Gulf coast. It is supposed that the enemy constitute an attack there. We have plenty left.

The health of our company is good   some little complaint but no one sick   we have a noble set of boys   can do more work than any two companies in the Regiment. We work four hours a day on the battery   We still keep up our prayer meeting. There is one kept up in Capt Brown's Company also

I have just learned that Willis Pyles is quite sick with fever. His friends made an effort to have him sent home on furlough but failed. They have succeeded in securing a room for him in town. This is a bad place to be sick. We still have plenty to eat but do not know how long we will have it   The supply of pork is about exhausted and we will draw rations of beef instead   I am afraid that we will become as tired of the beef as we now are of the pork. By the way tell Claudius to get my beef cattle in good condition. I suppose that Jessie is still with you I have not learned whether she is taking music lessons this session or not   I wish Dr Holmes to exercise his own judgment with regard to her studies   I wish you to be careful of her health. see that she takes exercise in the open air. I would like too for her to be with her sister as often as she can conveniently. I feel that I am greatly blessed in having my children where I need feel no uneasiness on their account. Remember me to sister Sarah and the children

Your afft Brother
Jas I Hall

Columbus Oct 3 [1861]

Dear Ma

Barnet Gracey will hand you this. you can learn from him more about our condition here than by letter. You wish to know something about what clothing I will need this winter. I have two good coats at home   My over coat and a black cashmere winter coat. I shall want two pair of winter pants dyed and a piece of woolen goods at home which if dyed would make a good pair of pants. They ought to be lined. I shall also want a pair of heavy cashmere pants and a warm vest   You may make the cashmere pants and send them up by the first opportunity. I can wait for the other clothing. I want if possible to get home some time during this month. If I do not succeed in getting a furlough you can send the other clothing to me. We are now on our new camping ground on the hill a mile from the river. have a good place, ground rolling enough to carry off the water. think it will prove a healthy place. have some sickness in camp now among your friends. my health is still quite good   We know nothing yet about our future movements. troops are still arriving here. Hardee is landing his command here to day. some of the troops have left. It is said in camp that a small force will be left in charge of the fortifications here and that the main body of the army will advance on Louisville. Do not know yet who will be left. We now expect to have a winter campaign. understand that Genl Johnson intends to drive the enemy out of Kentucky and Missouri. We are but poorly prepared for an advance movement. Our men must be supplied with clothing. shoes etc. from home. our tents are not suitable for winter use. We ought to have better   If our friends at home will gather a good supply of peas & beans they will be very acceptable this winter. vegetables of all kinds are very scarce in camp. We get a few stock peas occasionally   have learned to like them Give my love to the children. Tell sister Mary Eliza that I saw her father here yesterday. he has gone home   Tell Claudius that he must not think of joining the army   It would be self murder. He could not live through the winter. I will write to sister M.E. soon. Tell her not to become impatient but to write again

I have just received a note from William stating that you had both been sick but were better. hope that John will succeed in making up his company   Please write frequently   Write whether there is any news or not. the best news that we can here from home is to hear that you are all well.

From your afft son
Jas I Hall

Columbus Dec 15
61

Dear Children

Mr Munford will take this to you. I am quite well   weigh more than I ever did before. Uncle Robert & James are both well. We have had some cold weather but did not suffer with the cold. We have good thick tents that keep out the rain and wind. We have a big hole dug in the ground with a tent spread over it where we sit in bad weather. wood is plenty & we keep good fires

Our company got orders this morning to go back to the Regiment. we will go back this evening or tomorrow when we get out. then we will build cabins to stay in during the winter. The other companies in our Regiment have built their cabins and are comfortably fixed

We are working hard here   mounting guns & throwing up breastworks. We are not afraid of the enemy. If they should come down this winter we expect to drive them back.

After cold weather sets in I expect that some of us will get home for a little while. I should like very much to be at home Christmas but do not expect to go. I would like very much to see you. I expect that you have grown so much that I will scarcely know you when I get back. I am glad to hear that Jessie is a good girl at school.

You must not forget to take plenty of exercise in the open air, carry chips for Aunt Sarah & run in the yard when you are not in school. Sissy must be a good girl, obedient to Grandma and must talk loud to Grandpa. Jessie must write to me as often as she has an opportunity. Give my love to Grandma & Grandpa and all your Uncles & Aunts

Your aff Papa

Columbus Jan 16/62

Dear Parents

Mr. Young will hand you this. My health has been excellent until within the last two days. I have had cold with headache   am better this morning. It will wear off soon. We are comfortably housed in our Winter quarters. have an abundance of the best fire wood and upon the whole are getting along very comfortably   The health of the company is remarkably good   James Simmon has had a mild attack of typhoid fever. is getting better of it   has had no fever for several days. is a good deal prostrated. Recovers his strength slowly. will go home as soon as he is able to travel

We were somewhat apprehensive of an attack a few days ago. learned that the enemy were advancing upon us in large numbers. They have since gone back   probably on account of the severe cold weather we are now having the weather is becoming too cold for military operations.

I have pretty well given up all hope of getting a furlough this winter   should like very much to get home for a few days

I have been expecting Robt to come up for some days and shall continue to look for him   when he comes I wish him to bring my cotton mattress & some old comforts that I left in my room

I have not heard directly from home for some time   am anxious to hear from you   Give my love to the children. I hope they keep well

Your afft son
Jas I Hall

Memphis Apr 12 - 62

Dear parents

I am still here. Yesterday evening was so unfavorable that I thought it prudent not to go up to the camp   I have been to see our wounded have found them all doing well   I saw Mr Carruthers yesterday, he says that John was well. had been sick about had recovered   I have just seen Doct Vanderville, he does not know whether he will go north or not. If he goes Henry Simmon will give him fifty dollars in gold for John. I am as well as when I left home

My love to the children. I will go to Corinth this evening
Your afft son
Jas I Hall

Corinth Apr 22/62

Dear parents
I take the opportunity of sending this by Mr. Winford.
My health is now quite good. has been steadily improving
since I returned. The health of the company is not good almost all the boys are complaining   the sickness is caused
by exposure during and after the battle. We are in [a] bad
fix   It has been raining on us smartly for three days. This
morning however is clear & pleasant. I hope that it will have
a good effect on the health of our camp. We have no serious
case of sickness except that of Geo Calhoun. He is very
sick   I suppose you have seen the conscript law   I am
afraid that it will cause disturbance in the army   A great
many men say that they will go home when their time is
out. I hope though that they will think better of it. If the law
can not be enforced our country is lost. This is surely a
trying time. A large majority of our company will support
the law heartily. It is the only thing that will save the country and ought to receive the support of every man both at
home and in the army. I am sorry on Robt's account
I will be subject to draft under the law & will not be
able to take his place as I had hoped to do. I do not think
that he ought to leave home yet. the men here are all suffering with bowel complaints and he will certainly be sick
if he comes out now   Our boys lost most of their clothing & blankets in the fight & there is no chance of supply-
ing themselves here. They will have to get them from
home   as the weather will soon be warm they will not
need blankets so much as clothing
Give my love to the children & all the family
Please write soon
Your aff son
Jas I Hall

[To Mr. & Mrs. J.D. Hall of Mount Carmel, Tennessee
From Corinth, Miss. April 27, 1862]

This has been a sad day in our camp. Geo Calhoun died
this evening, a little before sunset. His father arrived here
early this morning. Geo recognized him when he came, but
was too far gone to talk to him. He is however comparatively
cheerful.

We received orders yesterday to cook five days rations and be ready for a march this morning. From some cause the order was countermanded. Our army is in bad plight for service. There is a great deal of sickness, mostly bowel complaints and not serious. We will send off some of our boys tomorrow. They will go somewhere down into Mississippi. James & Willie Holmes, John Haynie and Albert Templeton will go, none of them sick.

I am getting pretty well again. The weather yesterday and today has been clear and pleasant, and will, I have no doubt have a good effect on the health of the camp. In fact I believe that the sickness here is attributable to the extremely wet weather we have been having.

Our army has been largely reinforced since the battle [Shiloh]. Troops are coming in every day from all directions. We are hard at work throwing up breastworks. The boys work at it with a will, having felt the need of it in the late engagement. Our best informed men say that behind breastworks we can fight the enemy three or four to one. Our men are generally in good spirits since the fight, having completely routed a superior force of the enemy's best troops in an open field fight. We have had painful rumors today of the occupation of New Orleans by the enemy and of the consequent probable evacuation of Fort Pillow, but they are contradicted. The loss of the Mississippi River would be a serious inconvenience to us, but I have been fearful for some time that we will not be able to hold it. If Memphis falls into the hands of the enemy we will be cut off from all communication with home. That would be a hard trial but we must bear it patiently. I believe in the justice of our cause and that we will soon regain all that we have lost. I have no fear of the final result of this war, if the people of the South will only do their duty. We have the men and the arms to drive every scoundrel of the Yankees off Southern soil. All that is wanted is for the people to do their duty. If they do not do this they are not worthy of independence and have been arrant fools for undertaking the war.

Mr. Calhoun tells me that Robert[1] [Hall] speaks of coming up soon. I hope that he will not, he is subject to bowel complaints and would not remain well here three days. I received Robert's letter today. I do not know of any opportunity to procure a substitute. I think that he had better stay at home for the present on his furlough. If he can give a sufficient excuse for his absence which the state of his health will furnish, there will be no difficulty about it. I will see Capt. [Sidney E.] Sherril & Col. [John] Chester with regard to it.

I sent by Mr. Campbell for my old boots and a light cashmere coat. The coat I want for Junius [I. Hall, Co. C., 9th Tenn. Inf.]. When I came here I found him almost entirely absent of clothing—having lost it in the battle—and [I] gave [him] the light pair of pants which I brought with me. If there is a probability that communication will be cut off at any time soon, I wish you to send in good time, the clothing I bought in Memphis, my new hat and light shoes. I do not think though you need be in a hurry about it for the present.

Give my love to the children and all the family. Tell Jesse that I have been expecting a letter from her.

Your afft. son

Jas I. Hall

Apl. 28 It is rumored this morning that New Orleans has certainly fallen. If this be true we will soon have no communication with home by way of Memphis

Tupelo Miss   June 29. [1862]

Dear parents

Mr Calhoun will hand this to you   we were rejoiced to see him. had not seen any one from home since the evacuation of Corinth. Was glad to hear that you were all well. have felt great uneasiness about you. are glad to know that the Yankees have not been through the country & that the cotton has all been burned. It would only excite the stupidity of the Yankees & might lead some good men to do what they would afterwards regret. We long for the opportunity of expelling the enemy from the soil of Tenn. hope that it will soon begin in us. With the help of God we can do it & we will do it. It is only a question of time. Be patient. Before next fall there will not be a Yankee in our state. We are all anxious that our friends should under no circumstances take the oath of allegiance to the fed Gov. If the mass of the people will refuse there will be no difficulty about it. The few who take it will be doomed men. Of the final result of this struggle, I have no more doubt than I have of my own existence. We are bound to succeed. Our prospects are brightening every day. Of the army here it is not prudent for me to say more than that it is in better condition than it has been since the battle of Shiloh. The health of the army is excellent. the men are in good spirits and anxious to be led back to Tennessee. We have been gainers rather than losers by desertions. We are rid of a class of men who were utterly worthless in the army.

Within the last few days all men who are unfit for service have been discharged, so that we have now but the best & most effective men. As to numbers, suffice it to say, we have enough to whip the Yankees

We have glorious news to day from Virginia. McSillans [McClellan's] Army is totally routed, their artillery all captured   the army in full retreat with Johnson's [Johnston's] Army in close pursuit. There is no doubt of this. I do not know how long we will remain here. probably not long. I wrote to you a few days since by Mr McMullen. I hope you have read the letter. with regard to clothing, I can get along with what I have. My shirts are still good but if you have a good opportunity, I would like for you to send me the clothing I left at home. It is almost impossible to get any thing here. I recd a letter a day or two since from William. Tell him that I will write to him soon. Please write as often as you have opportunity. Tell Jessie to write. Give my love to the children and all the family

Your afft son
Jas I Hall

Humbolt May 7, 63

Dear Parents

Mr Calhouns boy will take this to you. I found our Regt here. The baggage had been brought back from Jackson. We have a nice dry camping ground convenient to wood & excellent water. The boys are generally well. Ed Elam & Mr Price are sick not seriously. When I got to the Depot this morning Mr Claiborne advised me not to bring up the box as every thing was in confusion here & I did not then expect to stay here   I have written to him to send them up tomorrow. Mr Sherill will go on to Henderson Station tonight I found Johns trunk at the depot and sent it out by John. Mr Sherill will inquire after the bed clothing

I gave the keys of the trunk to John   I also gave him my thin boots to take home. Ask Martin to oil them well &

have them laid away   My new boots are just such a pair
as I have been wanting all the while.
Give my love to the children and the family

Your afft son
Jas I Hall

Tupelo June 25 - 63

Dear Parents

I embrace an opportunity of sending you a few
lines   since I last wrote to you, my health has been quite
good. The boys are all in fine health except Jno W. Calhoun
who is sick at Durant   not seriously sick when last heard
from. We have a pleasant place for our encampment and an
abundance of excellent spring water. The health of the army
is very much improved since leaving Corinth. In numbers
in efficiency we are in better condition than we have been
since the battle of Shiloh. Robt Simmon & Manlius Hall are
here. Manlius has been discharged from the army. They will
probably remain with us for some time.

We are all anxious to hear from home. have not heard
anything directly since the occupation of the country by the
feds. hope that you have not dispared of the success of our
cause. I am afraid that a great many of our people in order
to escape annoyance will take that most detestable of all
oaths   the oath of allegiance to the fed government, I can
not believe that any of my friends will take it. I am needing
clothing I left at home & wish you to send it to me by the
first opportunity. Give my love to the children. Tell Jessie to
write by every opportunity

Your afft son
Jas I Hall

Vicksburg Aug 2 /63

Dear Parents

I arrived at this place day before yesterday from Memphis. had an agreeable trip down the river   had a passport & transportation to this place. have a passport from
this place to Mobile via New Orleans   do not know when
I shall get off am waiting for a boat going south   am stop-
ping at a private boarding house. I did not stop in Memphis
more than a few minutes as the boat was about leaving when

I came into town. I have gotten along so far very agreeably and am quite well. do not expect to be detained here long. Give my love to the children.

Your afft son
Jas I Hall

Chickamauga station
Oct/63

Dear Parents,

As I have another opportunity I will write a few lines Things remain unchanged here since my last. Am staying at the [illegible] four miles from Chattanooga was down at the Hospital yesterday   Our boys have all gone from there except Mr. Young who is still not well enough to be moved is suffering great pain from the wound in the elbow. sent a letter from Junius Hall two days since   He is at Marietta Ga in the hospital   Holmes Cummings & Jno Haynie all at the same place all doing well. I do not think that we will lose any more of the wounded of our company. I expect to be assigned to the command of the company in a few days. The health of the army is unusually good. the weather is cool for the season. We are getting along comfortably have good rations & plenty of it. have three days rations of bacon & flour & four of beef & corn meal in the knapsack.

As you will probably have an opportunity of sending some things to us soon I would like to have my woolen drawers, gloves, comforter, socks and anything else of the kind that you can send conveniently. I shall need a pair of boots & a hat. If the way is open, it would be well to send out all our clothing that is good & suitable of camp wear.

If you send Mark the Packages so that we can distinguish them. Give my love to the children. Tell Jessie to write whenever she has opportunity. My love to all

Your afft son
Jas

Atlanta May 30th 64

Dear parents,

I arrived here last night from the front. Am slightly wounded on the side of my head by a small piece of shell. Am not much hurt   Expect to be able for duty again in a few days   Will go down to Macon Ga tomorrow and remain until I am well. Billy Holmes came down with me. Has a slight wound on the knee. We left Robert Simmon at the field Hospital, severely wounded, shot through the side. I am afraid that his liver is injured. He is cheerful and is well cared for. He is too severely wounded to bear transportation in a wagon and will remain at the field hospital until an ambulance can be spared to bring him to the Rail Road. Our other friends are all safe. John was unhurt and quite well when I left the front. We have had a hard time for the last three weeks, have been fighting or marching almost the whole time. so far we have everything to encourage us. Our loss has been slight while that of the enemy must have been very heavy since Genl Johnston has compelled them to attack our breastworks in almost every instance. The army is in excellent spirits and has unbounded confidence in our General. He deserves it.

The religious interest in our Regt is still kept up. Quite a number have professed a hope since we left Dalton among them Jas Simmon. The good work is still going on   Truly

Informational marker showing Maney's Brigade in the first day's action at Chickamauga.

God has been good to us. His mercies are returned to us every day.

I saw John Carnes yesterday. have seen Bob Carnes several times lately, Billy Carnes is here in the convalescent camp, his leg has never healed up. Jas Carnes died a few days ago at Columbia S C   Joe Park was killed last friday— the day that I was wounded—Col finley, who married Miss Carrole was also wounded in the head not seriously. My love to all. I hav[e] not the leisure to write as much as I would like

Your afft son
Jas I Hall

pray for us

Camp near Marietta
June 13 - 64

My Dear Children

I expected to have written to you by Dumpty but was prevented by my wound. I came back to the Army yesterday. Have had a very pleasant time at the Hospital at Macon. I found some acquaintances there. Dr. Srum a cousin of the Misses Somerville was surgeon of the ward that I was in and was very kind and attentive to me. The ladies brought us a great many nice things   I met with Cousins Lizzie, Mary Eliza & Sallie Carnes who are all staying at Macon the last two going to school   After staying several days at the Hospital, I went out to the house of Mr Witherspoon the father of Sam Witherspoon who went to school to me at the Mtn. The family was very kind to me. I spent several days with them very agreeably. It was almost like being at home. I met with Miss Annie Johnston, who is staying at Macon. On my way back to the army   I stopped a day with Uncle Robt at Atlanta. He is very badly wounded and I am afraid that he might not get over, Uncle Jim is here and is well. Give my love to Grandpa & Grandma & all the family. I want you both to write to me

Your afft papa

Camp Near Marietta
June 13 - 1864

Dear Brother,

I returned to my Regt yesterday. Am entirely recovered from my wound. Was at the Hospital at Macon Ga. Met with kind friends   staid several days with Mr Witherspoon formerly of Memphis, Robt Simmon is at Atlanta. I spent a day with him as I came up. I am afraid that he is not doing well. The surgeon in Charge of the Hospital thinks that his wound is a very dangerous one. He is wounded through the liver and there is not much probability of his recovery. The boys here are all well. I saw John this morning. he is well. We are having a great deal of rain but manage to protect ourselves with blankets and oilcloths.

We have brisk skirmishing with the enemy day and night and are daily expecting a general engagement. The enemy are in our front in heavy force and I suppose that nothing except the incessant rains is delaying the fight. Genl Johnston expects them to make the attack. We are ready for them and with the help of God, we will give them a warm reception when they come. Our army is still in excellent spirits and confident of success. There is still considerable religious interest in our Regt   Jas Simmon has connected himself with the Christ—Assn. quite a number are anxiously seeking religion   We have prayer meetings when circumstances will permit

I suppose that Billy Holmes is making on home as he has a furlough of sixty days and has gone to North Miss. He will give you the particulars of our adventures since we left Dalton. I would like to send you some papers but cannot get them here. My love to sister Sarah and all the family   I will write to Jessie and Sissy   write when ever you have opportunity   We are extremely anxious to hear from home

Your Afft Brother
Jas I H

Chattahoochie river July 8 [1864]

Dear Children
Dumpy has just come in with letters from home. You don't know how glad we were to see [illegible]. We are now having a short session of rest for which we are very thankful as we now are having a hard time for some time past. At Marietta, we had a very difficult part of the line to hold. The enemy line of fortifications was within 50 yards of us. The firing between the two lines was constant day and night. On the 27th of June they charged our works, in some places seemed almost covered with them. Our loss was very slight.

I had no one hurt in my company and we had only two men wounded in the Regt.   no one killed. We had to move out very quietly when we abandoned our works but succeeded in getting away before the enemy discovered our movement. We are now south of the chattahoochie river, resting from our labors for a short time at least I wrote to you by Mr. McKall that I have seen your uncle Robt and did not think that he would get well. He died before Mr. McK- left Atlanta so that I suppose you heard of his death by him

Uncle John has left Atlanta on furlough and exalted to go home. I have not heard from him since he left but hope that you will see him before this reaches you. I am very anxious for him to get home. Your friends here are all well. My health since I came back from the hospital has been very good. The weather for some days past has been very warm and we suffer from the heat when we have to march in the sun. The country we are now in is well watered so that we do not suffer from thirst. We are doing well in the way of rations. have plenty of bread and meat, a little coffee and occasionally a few vegetables. How I would like to sit down with you to one of Grandma's good home dinners. It has now been almost a year since I left home and a long weary year it has been. I hope that before another year rolls round, if my life is spared, I can go home to stay. We all hope that this will be the last year of the war. I read Sissy's letter without difficulty and did not show it to any one. I am disappointed that she did not write again. she must write the next time. Thank cousin Abner for the nice knife he sent me by D. Give my love to Aunt Eliza and all my friends. Be good children and obedient to Grandpa and Grandma. I am glad that you are going to stay so long a time with them. I shall expect letters from you by Willy Holmes   May God bless you my dear little children

from your afft papa

CHAPTER 5

WARTIME CORRESPONDENCE OF
PRIVATE SAMUEL GLADNEY McCREIGHT

December 24, 1833–July 8, 1865

Harriet McDill McLaughlin was Samuel Gladney McCreight's niece. McLaughlin wrote a quite unique manuscript about her childhood during the war. According to her, McCreight's home was a rather large plantation in the Atoka area of Tipton County, Tennessee.

One early war-time letter fragment (not included here), states that he was the bandmaster of Company C of the 9th Tennessee Infantry. In the letter, McCreight sent home for his nephew (William J. McDill) to come and lead the band and to bring certain musical instruments with him.

Only one letter, and a portion of another, written by Samuel Gladney (called Uncle Glad by his nephew) McCreight were preserved in the family papers. This might have been due to Gladney's absence from the ranks. Gladney McCreight, legally, was replaced in the ranks by obtaining two substitutes but period correspondence suggests that this was an inexcusable occurrence. W. J. McDill wrote: "The Tipton girls ought to brand Uncle Glad as a deserter." He eventually returned to the unit and lost an arm in battle but evidently, the magnitude of his previous actions overwhelmed him, and he shot himself through the head shortly after the close of the war.

To sisters from Samuel Gladney McCreight.
Show this letter to all my sisters and brothers.

Columbus, Ky. Nov. 10, 1861.

Dear Sisters

I now have a few moments of leisure time which I shall devote to penning you a few lines to inform you all that I am still in the Land of the Living and enjoying good health.

Sisters, I will now attempt to tell you all about the Great and Bloody Battle at Columbus. It was fought on the 9 inst [November 9, 1861]. The Battle commenced at 11 o'clock and lasted till 5 in the afternoon. Gen. Pillow with Tappans, Wrights, Pickets and Nussels Regiment Numbering 2600 men was attacked by 8000 Lincolnites. The enemy had the advantage of us they were in the timber behind logs and trees. And our forces were forward in the open field. They fought that way for nearly 2 hrs. or until their ammunition gave out. The enemy seeing this made a charge on one of Tappans Arkansaw Regts. & one of our Batterys, our forces then retreated back under the Bank of the River. The enemy then had position of Col. Tapans Camp and one of our batteries. They turned our battery on us and fired all the tents in the camp. I have told you of the first two hrs. of the battle. During that time several hundred of our Brave soldiers were killed and wounded. In fact we were completely whipped say Gen. Pillow. But our brave Soldiers didn't know it. They rec'd more ammunition & c and were reinforced by 3 Rgt. of Gen. Cheatham's Brigade which was Smith's ? and Blythe's. These reinforcements were landed under a heavy fire from the Enemy. Gen. Cheatham soon got his men in to line he then ordered a flank movement which was to cut them off from their boats. At this time our big guns commonest poring their shells and balls in to the enemy which did great execution. The enemy then commenst retreating which was about 2 o'clock. Cheatham's Regt. pursued them on double quick time they overtook them in a cornfield & there is where we gained the victory. They were in close contact & our soldiers fought them with their bayonets and knives. There were 45 Yankys kild there in one pile beside the wounded. They were buried in one grave. I have seen that place. I did not see it until 2 da. after. It looked like a pen where hogs had been killed the Blood was thick all about over the ground for several hundred yds. around. The enemy at this place was completely routed and run like sheep

almost in every direction they dropped their knapsacks &
overcoats & haversacks & run like wild turkeys to their boats.
Our men followed them to within 40 yds of the boats and
fired several times at them while they were getting on the
Boats & after they were on the boat it is said there were as
many kild or probably more than there were on land.

Col. Logan who came back the next day with a flag of
truce to bury their dead acknowledged to Col. Wright that
there was 300 kild & wounded on the Boat he was on. Logan
also said that they carried off all their dead & wounded to
their Boats until they began to retreat. Logan says their
killed, wounded and missing is 1200. Ours is said to be 500
killed wounded & missing. We have 200 of their men prisoners, a Col. & several Capts. I went down to town this morning after the battle. I never saw such a sight. I could see
dead & wounded in every direction. They were still bringing
them over the River. I saw 9 Yankys dead & piled up on the
ground that had been brot over the river. A Capt. Broc(?)
who belongs to one of the Illinois Regt. found his bro. who
was Sergt. of Tappans & Ark. Regt. kild. He was killed by his
brothers Co. that is by the enemy. Mr Thomas the (?) told us
that he was on the Battlefield before the dead were taken
off   he said the dead and wounded were strewed for 7 mi.
A great many wounded were left on the field all night & were
found in hollow logs & treetops. I went over the River 2 da.
after the battle to see it. It was a terrible looking sight. I saw
a great many graves where the enemy had buried their dead.
All of our soldiers were brot over the River. The enemy were
burying their dead for 2 da. In one place the timber is torn
all to pieces. What I have told you I heard it from those who
were in the fight. Our Regt. was not in the fight. We were
formed in a line of battle & stayed until in the night. We
were formed the next day after the Battle till 12 o'clock. We
could hear the Roar of the Cannon & Musketry. I never heard
such a roaring. It was kept up for hours, a constant roaring.
Since I commenced writing a terrible accident happened.
Our big gun busted & killed 8 of our men, hurt Gen. Polk. I
must close I would have written sooner but hadn't time.
Write soon

Your affectionate Brother
S. G. McCreight
Co. C 9th Reg't. Tenn Vol.

(Addressed to)

Miss J.B. McCreight,
Portersville, Tenn.
Politeness of Mr. Wilkins

CHAPTER 6

WARTIME CORRESPONDENCE OF
SERGEANT JOHN RILEY McCREIGHT

1830–November 30, 1864

Third Sergeant John R. McCreight was the older brother of Samuel Gladney McCreight and the uncle of Scott, William and George McDill. John and Samuel Gladney had yet a third brother in the Confederate army. Osborne H. McCreight was born on September 9, 1837, and died on December 16, 1913. Osborne was a member of Company G of the 51st Consolidated Tennessee Infantry.

A deeply religious man, John McCreight was employed as a teacher before the war. Both of these elements of his personality clearly are reflected in his writings.

John McCreight was wounded in the 9th Tennessee Infantry's first battle on the fields of Shiloh. He participated in all of their campaigns and was killed while fighting at the locust grove near the Carter House in Franklin, Tennessee.

John McCreight was buried near the breastworks where he fell. His remains were marked with a wooden board which stated his name, company and regiment. He was reentered in April of 1866 in the McGavock Confederate Cemetery. His remains now rest there beside his nephew, William J. McDill, and their messmate, Al Templeton.

From J.R. McCreight

Shelbyville, Tenn, May 10, 1863

Dear Sister:
I was agreeably surprised on last Thursday to see S. G. in camp. He arrived here safe, did not see any Yankees on

109

his rout. I was truly glad to hear that the good Lord had blessed you so abundantly. I feel thankful that he has saved you all from the insults of those black bearded villians. It makes me feel more bloodthirsty every time I hear of those raids they are making on our country. I hope the day is not far distant when they will meet their reward. I rec'd the things you sent me I was very glad to get them although I could have made out for some time without them. I had 1 pr. pants 2 drawers and the shirts Billy gave me at Chattanooga and one that I had made in Ky. & one coat Capt. June Hall gave me two pr. socks when he came from Ala. He stayed with Dr. Sherrill and Mrs. Gibbs(?) formerly Sally Hall, until his wound got well. Sallie Fabrage sent me 1 pr. socks, 1 pr. suspenders & 1 pr. gloves by Scot and now with the clothes that you sent me I have a superabundance. The pants you sent were most too small from the fact that I am fleshier than I ever was   I weigh about 180 lbs. My health is better than it ever has been and the soldiers are in fine spirits and ready to meet Rosecrans at any time. We have glorious news from Va. We rec'd a dispatch from Gen. Lee the other day stating that the Lord had blessed him with another victory & that the enemy was in full retreat and that Stonewall Jackson was in their rear as usual. Gen. Paxton was killed, Gen. Jackson severely wounded, A.P. Hill and Heath, slightly. We have not received the particulars yet. The last account the enemy was retreating across the Rappahannock. We also have glorious news from Rome, Ga. There were 1800 Yankee Cavalry marching on that place. Gen. Forest got wind of it and he put out at double quick after them. he overhauled them, fought them five days, killed wounded & captured the entire command with a loss on his side of 10 killed and 40 wounded. I think this is the grandest feat of the war our cavalry is doing good work here. They are bringing in squads of prisoners most every day. There seems to be now no prospect of a fight here now that there was two months ago. I think the Yanks are getting tired of it.

Robt. Lemon, John Green Hall & Jno. Forsigh(?) arrived in camp last Friday from Camp Chase. They say that the Yankees are getting very tired of the war. They say that the Yanks wont stand the conscript. There is no volunteering amongst them. There is still a great deal of religious feeling in the army here and also in Va. A great many have professed and many are inquiring the way. On last Sunday I

stood on the banks of the Duck River amid a large crowd
and witnessed the emersion of ten soldiers. They formed a
line, took each other by the hand & marched in to the River.
There were a good many Ladies there to witness the scene.
After they came out of the water several of the Ladies came
up & extended the right hand of fellowship to them. There
are a great many things in camp life that tends to blunten
the sympathies and affections of our hearts, but when I witnessed the above scene I could not refrain from shedding
tears. On the evening of the same day in the 13 Reg T.V.
[Tennessee Volunteers], the ordinance of Baptism was administered to several by sprinkling. I hope and trust that
this good work will go on until the whole army becomes
religious and then that long prayed for boone will come
(Peace) which we all so much desire. I was very glad to hear
that Mr. Cummins was still preaching to you. I sent two
Rings by Uncle John Stevenson, one for Sister Margaret and
the other for Jane, the buttons & breast pin I intended for
you. I tried to get a gold pin to finish the breast pin but
could not get it. You can send it to Memphis and have it
finished to suit you if you choose, at my expense. I must
close I wrote to you last week by Henry McCain. My love to
all, I am yours until death

J. R. McCreight.

P.S. Tell Sister Margaret and Jane to write to me. My letters
are intended for the family. I can't write to each one sepa-
rately. I have a poor chance to write here. Scot went to see
Uncle Osy—he was on coast near Charleston when Scot got
there but had come home before he left. This is the second
time he has been called out. He belongs to the State Service, his family was well. Scot went to see Cousin James
McCreight. Cousin Nancy Morrison is keeping house for him
& Wm. B. McCreight's wife is also staying there. Scot said
Cousin Nancy is in good health & as cheerful as ever.

J. R. Mc- Sister, there are some little things I left out
which I will insert. I have a good pr. double sole Boots which
cost me $45.00 dollars, every thing is very high here. We
have organized a Christian Association in our Regt. The object of which is to advance the cause of our blessed Master,
to pray with & for each other, and to keep down vice and
immorality. We also have a vigilance & relief committee. Their
duty is to visit and relieve the sick, to watch over the conduct of the members & report any disorderly conduct of the

members to the association which will be dealt with according the 18 Chapter of Matthew.[1] We have President, Vice-President, Secretary & treas. Capt. J.L Hall is our President. I will not mention the other names as you are not acquainted with them. We meet every Sunday evening. We have prayer meeting every Sunday night. It is pleasant to meet at the close of each day to pray with and for each other and those at home which we love so dearly. I never forget you in my prayers. I ask of you never to forget me when at a throne of grace & if it is God's will I hope that we may meet on earth but if otherwise Oh, may we all meet around his throne in glory is my prayer. I must close. I would say to you, give my love to all and kiss little Amy for me.

(This letter is most likely to sister, Harriet McCreight Miller)

To Wm. Y. McCreight, Portersville, Tenn,.
from J. R. McCreight.

Shelbyville, Tenn. May 10/'63

Dear Brother:
    This is Sunday and I am seated on the banks of Duck River. I sent you a copy of the Chattanooga Rabble last week which had Bragg's official report of the battle of Murfreesboro for fear that it don't reach you I will give you a list of the killed and wounded on both sides. Our loss in killed and wounded 10,000, that of the enemy 19,000. We captured about 6,000 prisoners about 30 pieces of artillery and destroyed 800 wagons loaded with stores and ammunitions. We went in to the fight with thirty five thousand men and the enemy seventy thousand. I expect that you better hold on to the money that you have, and not pay out any more of it. S. G. said that Bibbs said nothing about the money I sent to the Wilson girls. I sent $130. by him, that was the amount on Billy Wilson's person when he was killed. I also sent a letter by him to the girls concerning his death, he was shot through the bowels, carried back to the river and died that night. From what I can learn he was perfectly resigned to his fate he said for his friends not to weep for him. I could find nothing about his burial, only that he was buried on the Battlefield. He was a Christian, a patriot and a Soldier. Oh, may his grave ever be green, may we ever cherish the memory of such men. Tell his sisters that I deeply sympathize with them in their sad bereavement and hope & trust

the good Lord may give them grace to sustain them amid this dispensation of his providence. His is done battling for his country he is gone to meet his reward. And Oh, may we ever have our lamps trimmed with oil therein ready to fall in train when the bridegroom comes.

I have nothing more that would interest you   Write & give me all the news, my love to all, I am yours until death
J.R. McCreight.

P. S. Gen. Vandorn [Earl Van Dorn] was killed the other day by a Doctor. I have forgotten the name—for being too intimate with his wife. No person seems to regret his death, the general impression is that the Doctor was justifiable in shooting him. I must close now and go to roll call. Write soon and give me all the news. I am your brother until death & c.

J. R. McCreight.

Later from Va.

Ten thousand prisoners captured, with a large train of wagons. The enemy retreating towards the Potomac. Our army has crossed the Rappahannock. Gen. Jackson's left arm has been amputated. The victory is complete.

CHAPTER 7

CORPORAL WILLIAM J. McDILL

1841–November 30, 1864

William J. (Billy) McDill went to war with his two brothers and three uncles—all in Company C of the 9th Tennessee Infantry. The middle brother of Winfield Scott and George Washington McDill, William was an accomplished member of the McDill family band.

Records show that he was present for duty from his enlistment until he was wounded at the Battle of Chickamauga on September 20, 1863—the battle which took the life of his little brother, Scott.

As evidenced by his letters that follow, William was a well educated, caring young man. The correspondence illustrates a love for his family, his duty and a marked admiration of the opposite gender.

After his wounding, William was furloughed and visited his aunt in South Carolina in order to recuperate. Upon his return, the army was still in winter quarters at Dalton, Georgia. Still unfit for hard campaigning, McDill assisted his comrades to the best of his ability with the wounded and other chores. He was witnessing and/or participating in the battles of Resaca, Adairsville, New Hope Church, Dallas, Rocky Face Ridge, Kennesaw Mountain, Peachtree Creek, Jonesboro, Lovejoy Station, Dalton, Decatur, Florence, Spring Hill and Franklin.

William J. McDill was one of the brave. As a member of General John C. Carter's Brigade of General John C. Brown's Division, he met death somewhere between Winstead Hill and the Locust Grove at the Carter House at Franklin, Tennessee. He, his uncle (John R. McCreight) and their messmate, Al Templeton, were killed within those five hours of carnage. Today they rest side by side among the 1,480-plus Southern patriots at the McGavock Confederate Cemetery in Franklin.

114

From W. J. McDill

Aceworth [Ackworth] Ga. May 22 '64

Dear Aunt:

Having nothing to do today I will trouble you by writing a letter. Perhaps you would like to know something of my stay in the Palmetto State. When I arrived there I was very much reduced and considerably fatigued by my journey— hadn't had my wound dressed in two days. I found Cousin Robt. Morrison at the depot. He took me down to Cousin James McCreight's, and as I went hobbling down the St. I met several boys, all calling me Cousin William. I didn't know who they were, but felt willing to claim kin with them. Before I had been in Winnsboro long I began to think I had as well call every body I saw Cousin. I don't have any objection to finding kinfolks when I am sick or wounded.

I went out to Aunt's, where I spent most of my time. I had to use crutches until the first of Feb. When I got so I could walk with the help of a stick, I felt quite proud. About this time I went to Chester Dis't to visit Hemphill Smith, and spent ten days with him, had the best time in the world —got acquainted with 18 girls, and several widows. I soon found that I would have to leave Chester or lose my heart: so I determined on the former—went back to F'field and spent my time studying arithmetic, grammar, and filling quills for the loom, and carding & c&c preparing myself for keeping bachelors hall. About the first of March Aunt Mary & I went up in the edge of Chester to see some cousins. I went to see some of the girls I had seen when there before; but beat a hasty retreat lest I should be captivated. On our return, I met up with Mattie Strong. She came to Winnsboro and spent one night with us. I visited most of our relatives, and had a pleasant time every where I went. The people, and especially the ladies, seem to sympathize with the wounded soldier. I believe cripples stand at or above par, thru-out the Confederacy. The Ladies of S. C. are very numerous & some of them quite handsome. They are very patriotic, but not more so than the Ladies of Tenn. Their patriotism has not been so severely tried as yours. I think the Tipton girls ought to brand Uncle Glad as a deserter, but spare his life as he will bring two substitutes with him.

We started for camp the 3rd inst. and left behind us many friends, and pleasant recollections, upon which memory will delight to dwell. It was almost like leaving home to me. We brot a fine lot of provisions for our mess, but the boys did not get to enjoy it long. They were ordered to the fight the next evening after we arrived. I was very glad to see the boys, but alas some who used to sit with us around our campfires are missing—the battle of Chickamauga has told its fearful tale. Friends, yes more than friends, a brother sleeps the sleep of death. Happy brother: what matters it now whether you lie beneath the blood stained field of Chickamauga, where hostile foot tread over thy grave; or rest in the quiet churchyard near home, where lies a gentle sister, and where friends could decorate thy tomb.

Since my arrival in camp, I have been with the boys but little. The army has been in motion for two wks, and I am unable to march far. I am now with the wagon train. I will now attempt to give you a full account of our retreat. The enemy at first seemed to threaten Dalton in front but finding our position too strong, he moved his forces to our left, 15 mi. Our forces were moved to meet him at Resaca a station on the railroads. Considerable fighting was kept up here for 2 da. The Yankees made repeated assaults on portions of our line, but our boys repulsed them handsomely. They then began to move accordingly. I do not know the position of the enemy at this time, some think they will continue to flank us, and compel us to fall back as far as Atlanta. Our army has fallen back about 50 mi. has repulsed every attack. No one seems to understand the move, or to know anything of Gen. Johnston's plan. He keeps his own secrets. The troops have great confidence in him, and believe he will defeat the Yankee army yet. Of course there are some who are a little gloomy. My own opinion is, that before long, the Yankee army will retreat much faster than they have advanced. Our loss is about 2,000 or 2,500 killed and wounded, while the enemy's loss must be greater, as he fought us in our works most of the time. Our Brigade had a skirmish on the 17th inst and lost several men, most of them from the 1st Tenn. Uncle John rec'd a wound in the left arm, the bone is not injured. He started for S.C. and I suppose is there by this time. Our Regt has lost 3 killed and several wounded. Jno. Wright of the 51st [Tennessee Volunteer Infantry] rec'd a flesh wound in the thigh. Uncle Glad and I are anxious to get home and stay until fit for duty. The longer I stay away the more anxious I am to get home.

May 30th. Not having a chance of sending this off, I write you a few more lines. I am now within 5 mi. of Atlanta with the wagons. The army is some 20 mi. from here, near Dallas and Powder Springs. Several fights have occurred during the past week, but no general engagements yet. Some three divisions of one army have been engaged, in which they repulsed the enemy with considerable loss. 300 Yankees were buried in front of Grantberry's [Hiram B. Granbury's] brigade, so says a man just in from the front. Our company was skirmishing Saturday, lost 4 men, wounded Capt. J.I. Hall in the head by a shell, J.P. Holmes in the knee by spent ball, John Sweet in arm, James Lemmon in the body dangerously. None of the wounds are dangerous except Lemmon's. We have heard from Uncle John he is in Winnsboro, S. C. says his wound is only a scratch. He is all right—will have a good time I know. I believe some of the boys are fond of getting slight flesh wounds, especially if they get furloughs by them. I do not care about any more furloughs if I have to pay as dear for them as for my last.

A letter from you would be highly appreciated. My regards to Aunts, also to Uncle Os and William.
Your nephew
W. J. McDill

To
    Miss M. R. McCreight, Portersville, Tenn.
Co. C 9th Reg't Tenn. Vol.

From W. J. McDill

Near Atlanta, July 9/64

Dear Aunt
    Your kind and interesting letter has been rec'd. You wrote like you were in fine spirits & good humor & rather disposed to plague me a little about the widow. I don't thin[k] you will ever have the pleasure of branding [illegible] me. You are mistaken about McL[illegible] girls—& Miss Martin instead of Miss Long. You say you intend to retaliate. I suppose you have a right to do so whether you have cause to do so or not. When I see you I will talk to you and tell you more about these things. I was amused at your account of the Yankee retreat to Memphis, & hope we may soon cause the Yankees here to do likewise. I will give you a brief account of the fight near Marietta on the 27th of June. The Yanks massed their forces & charged positions of our line of works held by Cheatham, Pleburn [Cleburne], and French's Division. Only 2 brigades of our division were engaged. Maney's, [illegible] and Vaughn's. Our brigade which was the posi-

tion of the 1st Tenn., the advancing columns of the enemy could not be seen until within about sixty yards of our works on account of the steepness of the hill and our works being some distance from the edge of the declivity. Our reg't was on the left of the brigade in an open field. The Yanks did advance in front of our reg't so it was ordered to move up the ditch and support the 1st Tenn. This they did firing as they went. The Yankees came in heavy force, prisoners taken say in five lines of battle, but they came only to bite the dust, to be captured, or to be sent howling back. At one time they succeeded in planting their colors on our works, but could not break our line. Some were killed on our works while displaying a gallantry worthy of a better cause than subjugation. The battle did not last long. The enemy soon fell back under cover of the ridge leaving the woods almost blue with his dead. In front of Claburne and French, he met the same fate. The loss of the division was very small, only 153, killed and wounded. This is the advantage of breastworks. At the time of the fight I was with Uncle Glad, near Atlanta. The next day I went to the front thinking I would be of some service to the wounded, but when I got there found very few wounded and they did not need my attention. I went out to the ditches & found our boys only sixty yards from the Yankee line and only 30 or 35 yds. from some of their sharpshooters. I thought this was rather close for a cripple to be getting, but concluded to stay with the boys as long as they were in that position, thinking that I could do as much fighting as any of them if they had no marching to do. The next morning (29th) after banging away awhile the Yankees asked permission to bury their dead under flag of truce. to which our officers agreed. Their dead had become very offensive, both to us and to them. The truce was a relief to us and also to the Yanks; for then we could raise our heads without being shot. A guard was placed between the lines to prevent the Rebs & Yanks from mixing too freely. Some of our officers went out and conversed with the Yankee officers while we privates stood and gazed at our blue neighbors. Some of the boys exchanged papers & traded with the Yanks, in fact both parties seemed quite friendly. As soon as the truce was out, the firing commenced again. We amused ourselves by throwing rocks into the Yankee trenches and shooting every time we could see a piece of a Yank. At night we would light turpentine balls and throw them to their works so as to see what they were doing. One man was killed and 2 wounded near me. I remained with the boys 4 da. The army has fallen back from Marietta to Chattahoochie River which is seven miles from Atlanta. I guess the move was caused by one of Sherman's flank movements, or perhaps Gen. Johnston thought this a better position. I hope the army will fall back no farther. Troops still in good spirits. Gen. Lee is still all right. Uncle Glad and I are still unable for active duty. We expect to go to the front to-day & stay with the boys till they move. No hopes of getting home this summer. We have just heard from Uncle John he is improving. Have you heard of Robert Thompson's death? He was killed in battle at kelly's Ford, Ark. "Friend after friend departs". Dr. John Simonton's wife of S.C. died recently. You spoke of getting bandages for our hospital; That is a good idea. You are always ready to lend a helping hand. Woman's devotion to our cause will shine in golden letters on the pages of our Country's history. I would like to be with you, to eat June apples & various other things. I hope and pray that we may soon realize the blessings of Peace and independence. My love to all my Aunts and Uncles. Tell the girls they are not forgotten by their humble servant, but he fears they have forgotten him. I am your Nephew.

W. J. McDill

Write often as you can.

WINFIELD SCOTT McDILL

December 29, 1842–September 19, 1863

Private—Company C, 9th Tennessee Infantry (Southern Confederates). Born in South Carolina, he was originally a member of Company G, 51st Consolidated Infantry but traded with W. B. Rivers of the 9th Tennesssee in April of 1863.

At the battle of Murfreesboro, the 51st Tennessee Infantry, except for Companies A, F & D, participated with Colonel John Chester in the charge of the 8th Tennessee regiment. Colonel Chester's report read—270 men engaged, 76 casualties, captured three pieces of artillery. The 8th Tennessee Infantry had 306 casualties out of 474 engaged.

In the battle of Chickamauga, the 6th/9th Tennessee Infantry lost over half of the 335 engaged. They were commended by General George Maney for valor. At 20 years of age, Scott was killed on the first day of the battle. While at the front of his company, standing on the breastworks waving his men to follow him, shrapnel from the enemy's artillery struck him down. Fifty-eight percent of the 9th Tennessee were killed or wounded in this battle. "He was buried in a soldiers rude grave upon the battlefield." His remains were later (1866) moved to the Confederate Cemetery at Marietta, Georgia.

This likeness was probably taken in January or February of 1863 (2 to 3 months before his death). He was slightly wounded at the battle of Murfreesboro as a member of Company G, 51st Tennessee Infantry, before he transferred to Company C, 9th Tennessee Infantry (April of 1863). Scott traveled to his aunt's home in South Carolina in which to recuperate. An artist lived with the family at that time. He suspended the ambrotype above a sheet of paper & projected light through it. The image on the paper was then traced and tinted by the artist. It is now in the possession of the Rexrode family near Winnsboro, South Carolina. They are descendants of the McDill family and reside in the same house that Scott visited during the war.

Winfield Scott McDill is the son of Captain Robert McDill and his wife, Nancy Wilson McCreight of Portersville, Tennessee. He was named after General Winfield Scott, who procured leave for, and thus saved the life of, the ailing Captain McDill during the Seminole Wars.

Winfield Scott McDill

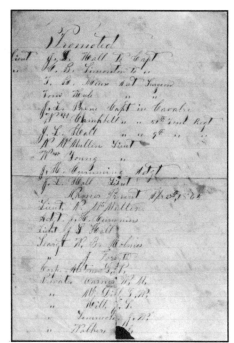

**George Washington McDill
1839–January 27, 1898**

This is the front side of a letter written by George McDill. He lists those promoted from Company C of the 9th Tennessee and the names of the original members present at the surrender.

**George Washington McDill
1839–January 27, 1898**

This is the reverse of the letter. Here, he lists the battles of Company C of the 9th Tennessee Infantry.

CHAPTER 8

Selected Obituaries of Officers and Men of the 9th Tennessee Infantry

JOHN W. BUFORD

Col. John W. Buford died at his home in Jackson, Tenn., Dec. 27. Col. Buford has been clerk of the West Tennessee division of the supreme court since 1884, a position he filled until his death. He was a native of Williamson county and was a graduate of the Lebanon law school in 1860. Shortly after he graduated, he moved to Obion county. When the war broke out, he joined the Ninth Tennessee regiment and was commissioned lieutenant-colonel and served until disabled by a desperate wound at Perryville. He took up his residence in Jackson after the war. Col. Buford was well known to all the lawyers of West Tennessee, all of whom had the very highest esteem for him. The old soldiers also had a high regard for him. All classes of citizens held him in high esteem, but these two classes of men were brought in contact with him most intimately and all of them were personal friends. He had been sick for many weeks and his death was not unexpected. There are many applicants for the position made vacant. Among the aspirants are E. B. McHenry and R. Black of Memphis, J. L. Goodloe of Trenton, Robert I. Chester of Jackson, John W. Buford, Jr., son of the late incumbent, and Horace P. Robson of Somerville. The office pays about $3500 a year.

GALLANT EX-CONFEDERATE IS DEAD.

George W. McDill Dies at His Home in
Little Rock, from the Effects of
a Wound at the Battle of
Perryville.

The body of George W. McDill was laid to rest in Mt. Holly Cemetery, Little Rock, Ark., last Friday, January 28th, 1898. His death occurred the night previous at the home of his sister, Mrs. Hattie E. McLaughlin, where the following day the funeral was held by the Rev. Mr. Foreman, pastor of the Central Presbyterian church of that city. George McDill joined the Presbyterian church at old Portersville in 1858, when he was a young man, under the ministration of Rev. Edward Green, and by a life of singular gentleness, purity and goodness, but wholly devoid of ostentation, he adorned the Christian character. His death, after many weary months of lingering decline and suffering, was the result of a wound received in the battle of Perryville, October the 8th, 1862.

He was born in Fairfield, South Carolina, October, 1838, and was therefore in his sixtieth year at the time of his death. In 1850 he removed with his parents, Robert and Nancy McDill, to Portersville (now Atoka) in this county. He was brought up to industrious habits, which never forsook him. He delighted to engage his energies, was the very opposite of sloth or idleness. His father was a merchant and offered him inducements to choose this as his life work, but he preferred agriculture; he loved the fields and the woods, birds and flowers—his dearest friend was nature. He was quiet and reserved even with intimate acquaintances, but in silent communion with nature his spirits arose to delightful animation and enjoyment. His goodness appeared by acts, not words, but his letters were all gentleness and affection.

He enlisted in Company C. (Capt. Wood's) of the 9th Tenn. Regt. Infantry in May, 1861, and surrendered under Johnson at Greensboro, N. C., April, 1865. Gentle, modest, kind and unassuming, as he was, if the writer were called upon to designate the best Confederate soldier he ever knew, the most unfaltering, loyal and devoted, without disparagement to the great, the gallant and glorious leaders of our armies, whose names eternal fame has rightly blazoned so high with the world's greatest commanders, he would place the chaplet on the brow of one who only was, and who only wished to be, a private in the ranks, and unhesitatingly name George W. McDill.

He not only did not shirk his duty, or falter in time of severe trial, but whenever volunteer details were called for, whether for work with pick and shovel while others slept, or as skirmishers to find the enemy's position and draw their fire, or for a desperate dash, it was his habit without the least semblance of parade to step to the front, and when remonstrated with by friends only quietly said: "Someone must do it; why not I?" and he did it. But he was not insensible to danger and fatigue, his heart was torn by other sad tragedies he witnessed. In a letter to his sister, recounting the incidents of the bloodiest battle of the war, perhaps, he says: "The battle of Franklin was one great trial of my life. Uncle John McCreight, brother William, Calvin McQuistion and Al Templeton, all killed. I was the only one of the old mess, that was in the ranks that was left. There were four of us that formed a file. Uncle John being tall, marched at the head of the company. We had stood side by side in hard fought battles and marched side by side in many a long march, but after the battle when we were ordered to fall into line and march on to Nashville, I looked around for my old comrades but they were all gone. I shed tears and wished I had died with them." He had seen his brother, Scott McDill, killed at Chickamauga and left him in a soldier's rude grave. He had experienced the terrors of Northern prisons, for twice, while wounded, he had fallen helpless into the hands of the enemy. He had an aversion for and shunned a hospital, unless to do acts of charity and kindness for others, as he would a pest-house. But when he was exchanged at Richmond, he was unable to help himself and landed inside a hospital, which he said afforded him a good bath and clean clothes, and praised the place but wanted to get away. And yet there was, perhaps, not a day from October the 8th, 1862, till the surrender, when he might not have had an honorable discharge by the mere application. At Perryville, he was reported mortally wounded, being shot through the body and through the lung, and ever afterward was pursued with a hectic cough and fitful fever, but a remarkable constitution and great resolution enabled him to overcome measurably the effects of his wounds and exposure, not only through the years of the war, but through the years of his subsequent life.

In 1872, enamored with the accounts of the fertility of the Neshoa Valley in the State of Kansas, he removed to Linden, but the winters being too rigorous for his impaired constitution, three years later he moved to Lonoke county Arkansas. Some six years ago his health having declined, he went to the home of his sister, Mrs. Robert W. McLaughlin, in Little Rock, Ark. Here he was offered the position of superintendent of Mt. Holly, the beautiful cemetery of that city. The care of the graves, the cultivation of the flowers, the communion with the dead in its walks and drives seemed to be congenial to his spirit and day by day, notwithstanding declining strength, he was at his post, until weakness confined him to his home thirteen months ago, since which time he calmly awaited the end, holding to the last his position of superintendent and watchful of its cares and responsibilities. The end was peaceful. Before he died he suggested that he be buried in the Confederate cemetery lot; that he would like to sleep with "the boys." George McDill never married. He was the last remaining brother of Mrs. Annie McQuiston and Mrs. Chas. B. Simonton, of Covington, and Mrs. Robt. McLaughlin, of Little Rock.

A GALLANT CONFEDERATE SOLDIER PASSES AWAY.

In the death of Capt. James I. Hall of the Mt. Carmel neighborhood, which occurred Saturday, January 29, 1910. Tipton county sustains a great loss, for his useful life was spent among our people whom he cherished always as friends.

Capt. James Iredell Hall, was born in Iredell county, N. C., July 24th, 1827. When six months old his parents moved to Hardeman county, Tennessee, moving in 1834 to Tipton county to the home where their family has always lived.

Capt. Hall was prepared for college by Dr. James Holmes at Mt. Carmel Academy, going from Dr. Holmes school to Centre College, Danville, Ky., in 1844, where he was graduated in 1847.

After returning home he taught at old Wesley, near Stanton, next at Hudsonville, Miss., then at College Hill, Miss., but his great life work was done at Mt. Carmel where he engaged in his beloved profession from 1853 until compelled by the infirmities of age to give up active life. This covered a period of about fifty years, broken only by four years' service in the Civil War. Of his record during these four years, his comrades with one voice proclaim him as one of the most gallant and intrepid who wore the gray.

He assisted in the organization of Company C, Ninth Tennessee Infantry. This company was largely made up of young men from his school. He pledged the parents of these boys to remain with them and to watch over them. This pledge he sacredly kept, refusing tendered promotions that would necessarily have removed him from the oversight of these young men. He was seriously wounded at Perryville and Chickamauga. At Atlanta he was left upon the field as dead. From these wounds he was a life long sufferer.

In 1849, Capt. Hall was married to Miss Sarah Lemmon, which marriage was blessed with two daughters, one of which, Mrs. T. B. Bailey, of Mocksville, N. C., survives her father.

His second marriage to Miss Mary Hall took place in 1866. Three sons were born to them, all of whom with their mother live to morn a most devoted husband and father. Of a religious nature, Capt. Hall early connected himself with the Presbyterian church at Mt. Carmel, and for about seventy years, made his influence felt as an active member and a devout officer of his church, also serving in the Sunday school in the capacity of teacher of the Bible class for young men.

He was laid to rest in Mt. Carmel Cemetery Tuesday afternoon at half past two o'clock, the funeral being conducted by his pastor, Rev. W. H. Perkins, assisted by Rev. W. R. Potter of the Covington Presbyterian Church.

A large concourse of sorrowing friends attended the funeral service showing the high esteem to which Capt. Hall was held.

MELANCHOLY SUICIDE.

A Returned Confederate Soldier
Blows His Brains Out.

A gentleman from Tipton County furnishes us with the particulars of a most melancholy occurrence near Portersville, Tipton County, Tennessee. Mr. Gladney McCreight, a respected citizen, who returned some time ago from the Confederate army, committed suicide on Saturday last. For some days previous to the one (last Saturday) on which he committed the rash act, Mr. McCreight had been suffering from an attack of low nervous fever. On Saturday morning he seemed unusually affected and retiring to his own room, he drew his pistol, and placing the muzzle to his head fired. The ball bursting his skull in a frightful manner, and scattering his brains about the room. The report of the pistol attracted the attention of his family and some friends who were present. When they reached the room they found Mr. McCreight weltering in his blood. Mr. McCreight was married about two years ago to a lady in South Carolina, by whom he had one child. Mr. McCreight was very much respected by all who knew him—a peaceable and quiet man, who never interfered in any way to disturb the quiet of the community. No reasons can be assigned for the deed, but it is supposed that he was mentally deranged at the time. It is a most distressing occurrence, and universally regretted by his friends.

Taken from the July 21, 1865
Issue of the *Memphis Argus.*

EX-CONFEDERATE DEAD

*From Tipton County, Buried at
Marietta, Ga., by the Ladies' Memorial
Association of that City.*

Editors Leader—The Ladies' Confederate Memorial Association of Marietta, Ga., long ago undertook to gather the Confederate dead from the battlefields of North Georgia as well as the victims of disease in area hospitals, and enter them in a Confederate cemetery at Marietta, they precarved the name, rank, etc. of every soldier where there was any means of identification, so that all graves may yet be identified. Of course there are many "unknown." This labor of love proved to be a Herculean test. There are from Tennessee alone 325 of these graves, 245 of them of bodies removed from battlefields, and 80 from the hospitals. The care of this cemetery and the preservation of these graves has passed to Kennessaw Chapter U. D. C., of which Mrs. R. L. Nesbitt, of Marietta, Ga., is the president. She was past president of the Ladies' Memorial Association which undertook the great work. They need headstones to appropriately mark these graves, and hard research has caused a complete list of Tennesseans so far as obtainable to be compiled and forwarded to the presidents of Tennessee Chapters of U. D. C., and other patriotic associations of this State with the request that headstones be furnished by these organizations of Tennessee to mark the graves of Tennessee dead. A complete copy of this compilation was published in the Memphis Scimitar of Saturday, June 29th. In this list, I find the names of a number of Tipton county's honored dead. Some of these graves I know have been searched for on the battlefields of Georgia, and were given up as among the unknown and undistinguished dead. The list furnished by Kennessaw Chapter, U. D. C., and published in full in the Scimitar, is the first information to many surviving relatives that the identification of these graves has been solved and the graves themselves kept clean.

Blessings on these patriotic women of Georgia for caring for our dead. Joe Brown Camp has Saturday appointed a committee to wit: J. J. Stone, H. J. Long and the writer, to confer with Baker Lemmon Chapter, U. D. C. and James R. Alexander Camp of Sons of Veterans, to raise funds to forward to Kennessaw Chapter, U. D. C., to mark the graves at least of all Tipton countians buried there as well as to mark the graves in Munford Cemetery. The names of the dead from Tipton county, so far as I recognize them on the compiled list, are as follows:

L. Kent, private, company C, Ninth Tennessee.
G. A. Dickens, private, company C, Ninth Tennessee.
H. C. Mills, private, company C, Ninth Tennessee.
W. S. McDill, private, company C, Ninth Tennessee.
Hector Marshall, private, company C, Ninth Tennessee.
A. R. Wilkins, private, company C, Ninth Tennessee.
R. S. Lane, private, company C, Ninth Tennessee.
J. B. Kirkpatrick, private, company E, Ninth Tennessee.
Geo. W. Locke, private, company G, Fifty-first Tennessee.
B. A. Barthalow, private company G, Ninth Tennessee.
Thomas J. Cole, private, company K, Ninth Tennessee.
H. X. McGuire, private, company G, Ninth Tennessee.

In the patriotic list of unknown Tennesseans, that are credited to the Fourth, Ninth and Fifty-first Tennessee regiment, and doubtless in this list are a number of Tipton countians. Let us see that all these graves are marked, and that the good women of Georgia, on expression of our deep gratitude.

Chas. B. Simonton.

TWIGS
Souvenirs of the tree around which the arms of Company C were stacked at the surrender. Brought home by George McDill.

CHAPTER 9

Brigades to which the 9th Tennessee Infantry was assigned.

April 6 & 7, 1862 (Shiloh)
6th/9th, 1st, 21st Tenn. & 7th Ky. Infantries—Under Colonel H. L. Douglas

June 30, 1862 (Reorganization)
1st, 6th/9th, 27th Tenn. Infantries & Smith's Mississippi Battery.

October 8, 1862 (Perryville)
1st, 6th/9th, 27th Tenn., 41st Georgia Infantries and Smith's Mississippi Battery.

(Murfreesboro & Chickamauga)
1st/27th, 6th/9th, Tenn., 4th Confederate Infantry, Col. Hurt's Tenn. Regt., 24th Battalion Tenn. Sharpshooters & Smith's Miss. Battery.

Nov. 25, 1863 (Missionary Ridge)
1st/27th, 6th/9th Tenn. 4th Confederate, 41st & 50th Tenn. Infantries & 24th Battalion of Sharpshooters. Maney's Brigade was in Maj. Gen. William H. T. Walker's Division.

February 20, 1864
Returned to Cheatham's Division.

Sept. 20, 1864 (Dalton to Atlanta)
1st/27th, 6th/9th, 34th/46th & 50th Tenn. Infantries. They along with Cleburne's Command, formed the army's rear guard.

129

(Battle of Nashville)   1st/27th, 6th/9th, 8th, 16th, 28th
                               Tenn. & 4th Confederate Infantries.
                               Commanded by Hume R. Field/Brown's
                               Division. Veterans state that their line
                               was not broken at Nashville and they
                               once again formed the army's rear guard.

Aug. 31, 1864   1st/27th, 6th/9th, 8th, 16th, 28th &
(Final Reorg.)   34th Tenn. Infantries & the 24th Battn.
                               Sharpshooters. They formed the 1st Con-
                               solidated Regt. Tenn. Infantry, Palmer's
                               Brigade, Cheatham's Division, Hardee's
                               Corps.

Interpretative Historians of Company C,
9th Tennessee Infantry
October 10, 1992

Photo was taken by Claude Levet utilizing an original process of the 1860's period. All uniforms and accouterments are based on in depth research of the Army of Tennessee and the 9th Tennessee Infantry in particular.

ENDNOTES

CHAPTER 2

1. Jeans—Jean cloth is a cotton-wool blend of medium to heavy weight which was utilized in the 19th century in the manufacture of common civilian work type clothes. Quite often called "homespun," jean cloth has a woolen weft and a cotton warp. Its origins are from Genoa, Italy—thus the term—"Jeans."

2. Commissary Jones—Edward W. Jones, born in 1825 in Tennessee and lived in District 2 (Holly Grove/Oak Grove) of Tipton County, Tennessee at a worth $700 in 1850. Company Commissary Officer; discharged on July 22, 1862, severely wounded at Shiloh. (Confederate Chronicles of Tennessee.)

3. Rev. D. H. Cummings—David H. Cummings, born in 1813 in Pennsylvania, and lived in District 1 (Covington/Leigh's Chapel/Rialto) of Tipton County, Tennessee at a worth of $300 in 1850. His wife was Emma H. from Alabama. (1850 Census of Tipton County, Tennessee.)

CHAPTER 3

1. J. D. Hall—possibly Jesse D. Hall, born in 1798 in North Carolina, lived in District 8 (Mt. Carmel/Clopton) of Tipton County, Tennessee. He was a farmer with a worth of $4,620 in 1850. His wife was named Rebecca and was also born in North Carolina.

   J. D. Calhoun—John D. Calhoun, born in 1805 in Virginia, lived in District 7 (Atoka/Brighton) of Tipton County, Tennessee. He was a farmer with a worth of $3,000 in 1850. His wife was named Elizabeth and was also born in Virginia.

   Robert W. Sanford—born in 1802 in Virginia, lived in District 8 (Mt. Carmel/Clopton) of Tipton County, Tennessee. He was a farmer with a worth of $15,506 in 1850. His wife was Frances Downs Small who was born in Tennessee.

   William Ligen—or William H. Liggon, born in 1800 in Virginia, lived in District 9 (Gainsville) of Tipton County, Tennessee. He was a farmer with a worth of $5,000 in 1850. His wife was named Martha and was also born in Virginia.

   John E. Stitt—born in 1815 in North Carolina, lived in District 1 (Covington/Leigh's Chapel/Rialto) of Tipton County, Tennessee. He was a farmer with a worth of $26,000 in 1860.

2. Mountain neighborhood—Mount Carmel is five (5) miles southeast of Covington, Tennessee. It was settled circa 1834 by members of the Old Bethany Presbyterian Church of Iredell County, North Carolina. The settlement was based around the Mount Carmel Presbyterian Church.

3. School house (Mountain Academy)—The Mountain Academy was founded in 1832 by Dr. James Holmes who later was the principal of the Tipton Female Academy in Covington, Tennessee from 1857 to 1868. This is reported to be the location of the organizational meeting of the "Southern Confederates" on April 23, 1861.

4. Captain Wood—David Josiah Wood was a Mexican War Veteran. He and James I. Hall were the principals responsible in organizing the "Southern Confederates." He was their first captain. He died on August 19, 1903, and is buried in Covington, Tennessee.

5. Camp of Instruction at Union City, Tenn.—Designated "Camp Brown," the men were garrisoned in tents and wooden huts in an area located about one-fourth to one-half mile north of the depot. It is said that troops were quartered in the area where Central Elementary School now stands and that a parade ground was located about the site of the Brown Shoe Company (the old building). From *Glory and Tears* by Rebel C. Forrester, H. A. Lanzer Company, Publishers, Union City, Tennessee, 1970.

6. 6th & 9th Tennessee Regiments—The 6th and 9th Tennessee Infantries were brigaded together in the summer of 1861 at Camp Blythe, New Madrid, Missouri and although retaining their own muster rolls, remained together throughout the entire war. The brigade was first placed under Colonel William H. Stephens of Brigadier General Benjamin Franklin Cheatham's Division. The two regiments were officially merged just prior to the battle of Murfreesboro.

7. Brigadier General Benjamin Franklin Cheatham—(October 20, 1820–September 4, 1886) Born in Nashville, Tennessee, he rose to the rank of colonel during the Mexican War and was promoted to major general of the Tennessee Militia. Serving as brigadier general early in the Confederate War, he commanded a division under General Leonidias Polk until after the Battle of Chickamauga when he was given his own corps. Shortly afterward, General Hardee was given Cheatham's position and Cheatham once again commanded a division. After the war, he farmed and served as postmaster of Tennessee in 1885. A very good recent publication chronicles B. F. Cheatham's life, along with the men of his command, entitled: *Tennessee's Forgotten Warriors*, written by Christopher Losson (ISBN 0-87049-615-8).

8. Colonel H. C. King's Kentucky Battalion—Colonel (then Major) King commanded a detachment of mounted rifles at Paris, Tennessee and was driven from the town on March 11, 1862. (From *Shiloh: Bloody April* by Wiley Sword.)

9. General Leonidias Polk—(April 10, 1806–June 14, 1864) Born in Raleigh, North Carolina, he graduated from West Point Military Academy in 1827. In 1841, he became the first Protestant Episcopal Bishop of Louisiana. He entered Confederate service as a major general in command of the Western Department, was replaced by Albert Sidney Johnston and given a division. He became a corps commander at Shiloh and rose to the rank of lieutenant general in October of 1862. Temporarily suspended after Chickamauga, he was re-installed and commanded the Army of the Mississippi in Georgia. He was killed by a cannonball at Pine Mountain, near Marietta, Georgia on June 14, 1864.

10. Randolph—Randolph is located about 35 miles north of Memphis (60 miles by river) on the Mississippi River in Tipton County. The population in 1861 was about 1,000 residents. This was the location of Fort Wright—a part of the early war river defense system and also a camp of instruction for many western soldiers. For more information on Randolph and Fort Wright, an in-depth study is available from the Tennessee Division of the Sons of Confederate

Veterans.—The Confederate Chronicles of Tennessee, Part 1 of Volume 3— (ISSN 0895-9455).

11. Battle of Belmont—Also known as the battle of Columbus, Kentucky or Columbus-Belmont, it was fought on September 9, 1861, from 11 o'clock until 5 in the afternoon. The 9th Tennessee Infantry basically dug trenches, reared redoubts and erected batteries in preparation for this battle. According to a letter from Samuel G. McCreight of Company C, 9th Tennessee Infantry, dated November 10, 1861, 2,600 Confederates were attacked by 8,000 "Lincolnites." These Confederates consisted of Generals Pillow, Tappans, Wright, Pickett & Nussel's regiments. Later 3 regiments of Cheatham's Brigade were sent as reinforcements. They repulsed the Federals, then the great battle was fought in a cornfield. It was said to be a Confederate victory. Colonel Wright returned the next day to bury their dead and said that he had 1,200 men killed and wounded. Dead and wounded were strewn for 7 miles. Some of the dead and wounded were found in hollow logs and treetops. Company C of the 9th Tennessee Infantry was not engaged. They were formed in a line of battle and remained until the day after the battle.

12. Injury of General Polk—As S. G. McCreight stated in his letter of November 10, 1861: "Our big gun busted and killed 8 of our men, hurt Gen. Polk." The cannon had misfired and became plugged during the battle. General Polk was supervising its discharge when the accident occurred. Many contemporary publications state that General Polk was not injured, but according to Dr. William M. Polk, captain, C.S.A. and son of General Polk, "during the progress of the battle a 128-pounder rifled gun had been charged while hot; but, no opportunity offering to use it to advantage, it was allowed to cool and remain charged four days. When fired it burst. This caused the explosion of its magazine, killing seven persons and severely wounding General Polk and other officers." This was taken from *Battles and Leaders of the Civil War,* Vol. I, page 356.

13. Double box house—Probably a dog trot house or some form of it.

14. Lieutenant Witherspoon, 6th Tennessee Infantry—The only Witherspoon found in the 6th Tennessee was Private John Witherspoon of Company G.

15. Fall of Forts Henry & Donelson—Union forces under U. S. Grant left from Cairo, Illinois on February 2, 1862. His forces consisted of 2 divisions under John A. McLearnan and C. F. Smith. Fort Henry was commanded by General Floyd Tilghman and Fort Donelson by Generals Gideon J. Pillow, John B. Floyd and Simon B. Buckner. Both battles were Union victories. Company C of the 9th Tennessee Infantry was not involved in either battle. More in-depth information on these battles may be gleaned from Volume One of the *Confederate Chronicles of Tennessee* and the *Official Records of the War of the Rebellion.*

16. Brothers John and Henry—Private John D. Hall of Company E, 51st Tennessee Infantry, and Sergeant Henry M. Hall of Company G, 51st Tennessee Infantry.

17. Battle of Shiloh—Company C of the 9th Tennessee Infantry marched 16 miles through mud and water on to the battlefield the night of April 6, 1862. They were held in reserve until 10 o'clock. They first successfully assisted General Breckinridge to dislodge the enemy from their rifle pits (The Hornet's Nest). Then General Cheatham sent the 9th Tennessee to assist Colonel Maney of the 1st Tennessee Regiment (The Peach Orchard). The 9th Tennessee was highly complimented for their charge by Colonel (later General) Maney. They drove them to their gunboats but sustained heavy shelling until dark. A train

of artillery divided the 9th during the night and caused them to camp on different parts of the field not knowing the whereabouts of the other. The next day, Company C fought in front of Shiloh Church through the entire day. (Here occurred some of the hardest fighting of the war.) Of Company C, 19 men were killed and 70 wounded.

The following is an account which was related by a member of Company H, 9th Tennessee infantry: "The Avalanche (Co. H, 9th Tennessee Infantry) maintained its organization through the second day's battle of Shiloh. About two p.m. on that day, an officer from the Washington Artillery, of New Orleans, rode up to our line and said, 'Gentlemen, my infantry support has left me. My battery is in danger of being captured by the enemy. Will ye not come and work my guns?' We replied, 'No! but we will support your guns.' We advanced on the double quick, as, also, did portions of the Hickory Blues (Co. G, 9th Tennessee Infantry), from Districts Number Seven and Number Sixteen of Obion County, and the Southern Confederates (Co. C, 9th Tennessee Infantry), from Covington. As we advanced, we met a regiment from Louisiana, on the retreat. Their jackets were turned inside out. As we were passing them, Gen. Beauregard and members of his staff rode up. Beauregard addressed the Louisiana regiment in French. They hurrahed. Beauregard and his staff rode off and the Louisianans kept on retreating, while the Avalanche and portions of the other two companies of Tennesseans kept on advancing until they reached the battery and pulled it out by hand and saved it, the artillery horses all having been killed."

In the two-days' fight, the regiment lost 60 men and retreated until 9 o'clock, halted and slept in a heavy rain. They reached Corinth on the next day were they remained for 7 weeks. Company C's silk first national flag was used as the regimental standard for the 9th regiment. Their brigade consisted of the 6th/9th, 1st/27th Tennessee and the 7th Kentucky Infantries under Colonel William H. Stevens. After the reorganization at Corinth, their brigade consisted of the 1st/27th, 6th/9th Tennessee Infantries and Smith's Mississippi Battery.

18.   Robert Lemmon—He was originally elected third lieutenant of Company C, 9th Tennessee Infantry. He was not re-elected at the reorganization in May 1862 at Corinth, but served as a private soldier throughout the remainder of his life. He was wounded and captured at the battle of Perryville, exchanged and rejoined his comrades. Mortally wounded at the battle of Dallas, Georgia, he was shot through the liver and died at the hospital in Atlanta, buried in the hospital graveyard and later removed to the Mount Carmel cemetery in Tipton County, Tennessee. He had his discharge papers in his pocket at the time of his death.

After the war, Captain James I. Hall had him re-interred beside the grave of his own father with his wife, Mary Hall, on the other side and Captain Hall to her left. To bury him between his own father and wife is the ultimate gesture of love for his former student and fellow soldier—in death, to make him a part of his own family!

19.   General Chalmers—James Ronald Chalmers was born in Halifax County, Virginia and practiced law in Holly Springs, Mississippi. Early in the war, he was appointed colonel of the 9th Mississippi Infantry and commanded at Pensacola, Florida. He fought at Shiloh, in Kentucky and at Murfreesboro. Being transferred to the cavalry, he commanded a division under N. B. Forrest in which he took part in the brilliant raids in northern Mississippi, west Tennessee and Kentucky. After the war, General Chalmers was thrice elected to congress for

the state of Mississippi. In 1888, he moved to Memphis, Tennessee and practiced law there until his death on April 9, 1898.

20. Battle of Munfordsville, Kentucky—September 17, 1862—It was here that General Bragg captured a 4,000-man Federal garrison under Colonel John T. Wilder by convincing him that he was surrounded and outmanned.

21. Centre College—Founded in 1819 by Presbyterians who were eager for an educated clergy and educated people to teach their children, they opened their doors in the fall of 1820 with a faculty of 2 and student body of 5. Under the presidency of Dr. John C. Young in the later part of the 1830–1857 era, Centre College advanced to a position among the highest ranking colleges in America. Centre College alumni have included 2 U.S. vice presidents, one chief justice of the U.S., an associate justice of the Supreme Court, 13 U.S. senators, 43 U.S. representatives, 10 moderates of the Grand Assemblies of the Presbyterian Church and 11 governors. (From the 1992–1994 Centre College Catalog, Vol. CLXV, published by Centre College; Danville, Kentucky.)

22. Battle of Perryville—According to the regimental history in Lindsley's Annals, one fourth of the regiment were casualties. On October 8, 1862, "it made its best fight during the war; it went into the first and thickest of the fight. In the first charge, it captured a section of artillery by which Major General Jackson and Brigadier General Terrill of the Federal Army lay dead." Fifty-two men were killed and seventy-six were wounded of the regiment. A definitive victory for the South was obtained and then lost due to poor generalship. The brigade in this battle consisted of the 1st/27th, 6th/9th Tennessee, 41st Georgia Infantries and Smith's Mississippi Battery.

23. General Buell—(March 23, 1818–November 19, 1898) Major General Don Carlos Buell was born in Marietta, Ohio and served in the Mexican War. He graduated from West Point in 1841. He was replaced after the Kentucky Campaign by Major General Rosecrans and tried by a formal court-martial. He resigned from the army on June 1, 1864, and became president of the Green River Iron Company.

24. Colonel Buford—Lieutenant Colonel John W. Buford was originally captain of Company H, 9th Tennessee Infantry—the "Obion Avalanche"—Men from Troy County.

25. Major Kelso—Major G. W. Kelso, 9th Tennessee Infantry.

26. Captain Irby—Captain Henry C. Irby, Company D, 9th Tennessee Infantry.

27. Goodnight farm—or Goodknight—Located less than one mile from the area of Cheatham's attack, it served as a Confederate hospital after the battle. An undetermined number of unknown Confederates are buried in a plot near the site of the Goodknight house. (From Blue and Gray magazine, October–November, 1983 "The General's Tour.")

28. Will Carnes—Private William N. Carnes of Company C, 9th Tennessee Infantry, was wounded at Perryville, captured and exchanged. He was paroled at Greensboro, North Carolina at the end of the war.

Maynard carbine—At a length of 36.63 inches and weighing only 6 lbs., the .50 caliber Maynard carbine was one of the most accurate breech-loading carbines produced during the war. Employing an operating lever/trigger guard, a metallic cartridge with an extra wide base was ignited by means of a standard percussion cap. (From An Introduction to Civil War Small Arms by Earl J. Coates and Dean S. Thomas, 1990 by Thomas Publications, Gettysburg, Pennsylvania.)

29. General Zollicoffer—(May 19, 1812–January 19, 1862) Brigadier General Felix Kirk Zollicoffer was born in Maury County, Tennessee. He was a printer and editor and served in the Seminole War. He was elected to Congress from 1853 to 1859. In an odd quirk of fate, Congressman Zollicoffer, in 1859, opposed Sam Colt's extension of his basic patent of revolving pistols. Zollicoffer was killed by the Union Colonel (later General) Fry of the 4th Kentucky Regiment with an early model, 8-inch fluted 4-screw Colt Army revolver on January 19, 1862, at Mill Springs, Kentucky.

30. Union General Boyle—Brigadier General Jeremiah T. Boyle was the military Commandant of Kentucky. (From *Perryville: Battle for Kentucky* by Kenneth A. Hafendorffer.)

31. Colonel Stitts Place—Called the battle of Lemmons Woods, located near the present site of Tipton County Memorial Gardens (Cemetery). At noon on March 9, 1863, 150 Confederates under Colonel Richardson of the 12th Tennessee Cavalry were attacked by approximately 1,000 Federals of the 6th and 7th Illinois Cavalry along with a 6 gun battery under the command of Colonel Grierson. The next day, he met a detachment of 300 men from the 7th Kansas and 4th Illinois Cavalries under the command of Lieutenant Colonel Martin Wallace. According to Richardson's report, he had 2 men killed, 5 wounded with 8 prisoners while the Union casualties were 7 killed, 6 wounded and 20 taken prisoners. The Union casualty report was quite different but also reported of very few casualties. Though a mere skirmish, it was the only engagement of any size fought in Tipton County, Tennessee.

32. Irving Block—The Irving Block was a notorious Federal prison located on modern day North Main Street between Jefferson and Court streets in Memphis, Tennessee. Both men and women were detained there. It was intended to be a prison for their own prisoners. Operating between 1862 and 1865, the conditions were so wretched that Abraham Lincoln himself ordered an inquiry and later abolished it.

33. Tom Norwent—Only a Private Thomas H. Norvell of Company G, 6th Tennessee Infantry, could be found in the records.

34. Captain J. V. Locke—Tennesseans in the Civil War list J. B. Locke as captain of Company E, 9th Tennessee Infantry.

35. Battle of Chickamauga—Fought on September 19 and 20, 1863. The regiment was hotly engaged on the first day and sustained great loss. In both days' fighting, the regiment sustained 35 men killed and 40 wounded (one fifth of the total engaged). The brigade consisted of members of the 1st/27th, 6th/9th Tennessee, 4th Confederate Infantries, Colonel Hurt's Tennessee Regiment, 24th Battalion of sharpshooters and Smith's Mississippi Battery.

36. Battle of Missionary Ridge—According to the regimental history, on September 22, 1863: "Our line charged up these rugged and rocky heights with a courage that spurned the natural impediments, throwing themselves with a charge bayonet against the foe with such impetuosity that they fled pell-mell down the other side of the ridge, leaving many prisoners in our hands." In this charge, the 9th had no one killed but a few wounded. On November 25 and 26, 1863, the 9th fought under protection in this battle and sustained no loss save a few prisoners. Once again, the 9th brought up the rear.

37. The Craven Place—This is the home of Robert Cravens on Lookout Mountain, Tennessee. It was badly damaged in the "Battle above the Clouds." The first line of Confederate works ran parallel to the Cravens house, and the second

line was a quarter mile behind it. Cravens later built an improved house on the same foundation as the original. Today, this improved house is maintained by the Park Service. (*Battlefields of the Civil War* by Roger W. Hicks and Frances E. Schultz, 1989 BLA Publishing Ltd. ISBN 0-88162-400-4.)

38. Battle Above the Clouds—Also known as "the Battle of Lookout Mountain," here, General Hooker scaled the face of the mountain to obtain a substantial Union victory. The battle was not actually above the clouds, instead, was fought in a dense fog. According to Private T. J. Walker of the 9th Tennessee: "Prior to the Battle of Chickamauga, there weren't a dozen Confederate soldiers on the mountain when Hooker made his celebrated charge above the clouds. That monument at Point Lookout is all fuss and feathers."

39. Cheatham's Mixed Division—Of General B. F. Cheatham's entire Tennessee Division, only Marcus J. Wright's Brigade remained. They were composed of the 8th, 16th, 28th, 38th, and 51st Tennessee Regiments, 22nd Battalion plus Carne's Battery. The other 17 Tennessee Regiments were scattered. The 1st/27th, 6th/9th, 41st/50th Tennessee Regiments, 4th Confederate Regiment, 24th Battalion of Sharpshooters and Maney's Brigade were now placed in William H. T. Walker's Division.

40. Battle of Cat Creek—November 27, 1863—This was a small rear guard battle fought after leaving Chickamauga Station. General Maney was wounded in that battle.

41. Dalton—It was at this location that the Army of Tennessee positioned their winter quarters for four months in 1863. According to the regimental history: "It was here that every man in the 6th and 9th Tennessee reenlisted for the war. The other regiments followed their example. It was also here that a tree fell, silently, on ten men during a prayer service, killing all of them. At this time (from Dalton to Atlanta) the brigade consisted of the 1st/27th, 6th/9th, 34th/46th and 50th Tennessee Infantries. This brigade along with Cleburne's Brigade formed the rear guard."

42. General Joseph E. Johnson—Joseph Eggelston Johnston (misspelled by many veterans) acquired leadership of the Army of Tennessee in May of 1864.

43. General Walker's Division—The brigades of General William H. T. Walker consisted of the 1st/27th, 6th/9th, 41st and 50th Tennessee, 4th Confederate Infantries and the 24th Battalion of Sharpshooters.

44. Battle of Rocky Face Ridge—May 7, 1864—Rocky Face Ridge is a mountain range in the Dalton, Georgia area. Here, Sherman outflanked Johnston's Confederates and forced his retreat from Dalton. These were a series of battles at Dug Gap, Mill Creek Gap, etc., from May 7th until the 12th.

45. Whitworth rifle—At a length of 48.75 inches and weighing almost 10 pounds, the British Whitworth rifle looks very much like the pattern 1853 Enfield rifle. The .45 caliber hexagonal bore Whitworth proved to be one of the most accurate sniper rifles with killing accuracies at ranges up to 1,800 yards. It was a favorite arm of the Confederate sharpshooter and saw service in both eastern and western theaters.

46. Battle of Resaca—May 15, 1864—Tactically a drawn battle, both sides made two attacks which amounted to little, but strategically, it was a great Union victory. The Union lost 4,000 and the Confederates lost 3,000 effectives. Here, Sherman once again forced Johnston out through the use of flank movements. It was here that the 9th Tennessee Regiment lost its only officer from Dalton to Atlanta—Lieutenant John Tally of Company K.

47. Captain Rice—No information on a Captain Rice can be obtained that would have been in the same brigade; however, there was a 2nd Lieutenant Thomas H. Rice in Company K, 6th Tennessee Regiment.

48. Pontoon Bridge over the Oostanaula River—This was the route taken by Maney's Brigade in quick evacuation of Resaca. A pontoon bridge is a series of boats strung together with boards or planks placed over them to form a temporary road over which an army can cross. This was meant to be temporary as the bridges here were burned behind them as the army withdrew southward through Calhoun. (*Tennessee's Forgotten Warriors* by Christopher Losson 1989 by the University of Tennessee Press/Knoxville.)

49. Battle of Adairsville—May 17, 1864—This was the battle in which Sam Watkins, in his book *Co. Aytch*, described their fight in the Octagon house. Here the 9th Tennessee Infantry was posted across an open field from the enemy behind Turner's Mississippi battery.

50. Battle of Dallas—May 27, 1864—It was here that General John C. Breckinridge led his troops in a frontal assault across an open field. They planted their flag on the Federal breastworks but couldn't hold it. Later they marched back to the battlefield of the previous day—New Hope Church.

51. Mountain graveyard—This is the burying ground of the Mount Carmel Church in Tipton County, Tennessee.

52. Battle of Kennesaw Mountain—(Dead Angle or Dead Point) June 27, 1864—General Maney's Brigade, of which the 9th was a member, bore the brunt of this battle. General William T. Sherman's men charged up Cheatham's Hill into a massive fire. At this point, the breastworks were constructed to the rear of the actual crest of the hill, thus causing a safe area for the Federals. They dug a tunnel, expecting to "blow up" the Confederate breastworks with explosives, but the works were abandoned the day before the planned explosion. Sherman outflanked Johnston's army, causing another retreat.

53. Battle of Peach Tree Creek—July 20, 1864—Here, General Hood planned to attack Union General Thomas as he crossed Peach Tree Creek. Confusion ensued and Hood's plan went awry. Divisions became separated and attacks were piece-meal. Maney's Division, of which the 9th Tennessee was a member, was the only full division that made contact with the enemy.

54. Battle of Decatur—Battle of Atlanta—July 22, 1864—According to the regimental history listed in Lindsley's Annals, the 9th Tennessee Regiment lost one-fifth of its number in this engagement. It was here that Captain J. L. Hall, Lieutenants Jesse Ferrill, Gabe Robinson, and W. H. Morgan were killed.

55. Sloughing—separating of dead tissue from living tissue.

56. Dr. Westmorland—There was a Dr. Willis F. Westmoreland of the Atlanta Medical College Hospital that received praise for his successful demonstrations in behalf of conservative surgery.

CHAPTER 4

1. Robert Hall—Sergeant of Company G, 51st Tennessee Infantry.

CHAPTER 6

1. 18th Chapter of Matthew—Verses 15 and 16 state: "Moreover if thy brother shall trespass against thee, go and tell him his fault between thee and him alone: if he shall hear thee, thou hast gained a brother. But if he will not hear thee, then take with thee one or two more, that in the mouth of two or three witnesses every word may be established."

PHOTOGRAPHIC CREDITS

1. Reunion of Company C, 9th Tennessee Infantry—Debbie Williams/Russell Bailey Collection.
2. Souvenir walking stick from Surrender Tree—Private Collection of the Author.
3. Captain Charles Bryson Simonton—Private Collection of Russell B. Bailey.
4. Captain Charles Bryson Simonton (In Later Life)—Private Collection of the Author.
5. The First National Flag of the Southern Confederates—Private Collection of the Author.
6. Clopton's Campground—Private Collection of the Author.
7. Thomas J. Walker—Mrs. T. J. Walker III.
8. Ensign Robert H. Gibbs—Military Annals of Tennessee.
9. Brigadier General Speed Smith Fry—Curtis Cox Collection.
10. Rev. D. H. Cummings—Mount Carmel Church Collection.
11. Position marker of the 6th/9th Tennessee Infantry on Chickamauga Battlefield—Private Collection of the Author.
12. Private David H. Haynie—Collection of the City of Covington, Tennessee, Russell Bailey, Mayor.
13. Dalton Issue Flag of the 6th and 9th Tennessee Infantry— David Gwinn Collection.
14. Captain James Iredell Hall—Private Collection of Mrs. Nell Christopherson.
15. Mount Carmel Presbyterian Church—Private Collection of the Author.
16. Camp Beauregard Historical Marker—Private Collection of the Author.

17. Brigade Marker—Informational Marker at Chickamauga Battle-field—Private Collection of the Author.

18. Winfield Scott McDill— Rexrode family of Winnsboro, S.C.

19. "Promotions"—Note written by George W. McDill—Private Collection of the Author.

20. "Engagements"—Note written by George W. McDill—Private Collection of the Author.

21. Souvenir Twigs from Surrender Tree—Private Collection of the Author.

22. Company C, 9th Tennessee Infantry (Modern Interpretative Historians)—Claude Levet Collection.

BIBLIOGRAPHY

Allen, Penelope Johnson. *Tennessee Soldiers in the Revolution.* Bristol, Tennessee, The Tennessee Society, Daughters of the American Revolution, 1935.

Carpenter, V. K. *Seventh Census of the United States, 1850, Tipton County, Tennessee.* Reprinted by Mrs. Leister E. Presley. Searcy, Arkansas, 1979.

Carpenter, V. K. *Eighth Census of the United States, 1860, Tipton County, Tennessee.* Reprinted by Mrs. Leister E. Presley. Searcy, Arkansas, 1979.

Cavanaugh, John. *Historical Sketch of Obion Avalanche, Company H, Ninth Tennessee Infantry, Confederate States of America.* Union City, Tennessee: The Commercial, 1922.

Coates, Earl J. and Dean S. Thomas. *An Introduction to Civil War Small Arms.* Gettysburg, Pennsylvania: Thomas Publications, 1990.

Connelly, Thomas Lawrence. *Autumn of Glory, The Army of Tennessee, 1862–1865.* Baton Rouge and London: Louisiana State University Press, 1971.

Cummingham, H. H. *Doctors in Gray: The Confederate Medical Service.* Baton Rouge and London: Louisiana State University Press, 1958, 229.

Daughters of the American Revolution. *Tipton County Cemetery Tombstone Inscriptions.* Unpublished manuscript, October 1974.

Edwards, William B. *Civil War Guns.* Harrisburg, Pennsylvania: Stackpole Co., 1962, 325.

Forrester, Rebel C. *Glory and Tears.* Union City, Tennessee: H. A. Lanzer Company, 1970.

Hafendorfer, Kenneth A. *Perryville: Battle for Kentucky.* Louisville, Kentucky: KH Press, 1991.

Hicks, Roger W. and Frances E. Schultz. *Battlefields of the Civil War.* East Grinstead, Sussex, England: BLA Publishing Ltd., 1989.

The Holy Bible, King James Version, St. Matthew, Chapter 18, verses 15 and 16.

Horn, Stanley F. *The Army of Tennessee.* Indianapolis, Indiana: The Bobbs-Merrill Company, 1941.

Losson, Christopher. *Tennessee's Forgotten Warriors, Frank Cheatham and his Confederate Division.* Knoxville, Tennessee: The University of Tennessee Press, 1989.

McMurray, W. J. *History of the Twentieth Tennessee Regiment Volunteer Infantry C.S.A.* Nashville, Tennessee: The Publication Committee, 1904.

Shakespeare, William. *The Complete Works of William Shakespeare.* Dallas and Houston, Texas; Oakland, California; and Lithia Springs, Georgia: Amaranth Press, 1987.

Sweet, S. E. *Confederate Reminiscences and Roster of Company C, Ninth Tennessee Volunteer Infantry Regiment.* Compiled by William Young and Joseph Forsythe, Private printing, n.d.

Sword, Wiley. *Shiloh: Bloody April.* Dayton, Ohio: Morningside House, Inc., 1974.

The Editors of "The Century." *Battles and Leaders of the Civil War.* New York: The Century Company, November 1887.

"The General's Tour." *Blue and Gray Magazine,* vol. 1, issue 2 (October–November 1983). Ed. David E. Roth, 21, 44.

The Historical Records Survey Transcript Unit (W.P.A.). *Tennessee Records of Tipton County Will Book 1824–1859.* Nashville, Tennessee: Nashville Historical Records Survey, February 3, 1939.

Watkins, Sam R. *"Co. Aytch," a Side Show of the Big Show.* New York: Macmillan Publishing Co., 1882.

INDEX

A

Adairsville, battle of, xix, 67, 114, 139
Adams, Benjamin, 9
Aeneid, Virgil's, 81
Alabama, xi, xxiii, 110, 132
    Demopolis, xxiii, 61–62
        Marian, 62
    Meridian, xxiii
    Mobile, xv, 28, 48, 100
        citizens of, 28
    Montgomery, xv, xxiii, 28, 48, 60–61
    Selma, xxiii
Alabama Regiment, 30
Alabama River, 48
Allen, Private John, 3
Allen, Sam, 44
American Tract Society, 41
Anderson, James Robert, 55
Arkansas, 2
    Forrest City, 2
    Kelly's Ford, 119
    Little Rock, 123, 124–25
        Central Presbyterian Church, 123
    Lonoke County, 124
Arkansas Regiment, 25
Army of Tennessee, xxi, xxiii, 138
Army of the Mississippi, 133
Army of the Ohio, xxi
Associate Justice of Supreme Court, 136
Atlanta, battle of, xx, 75–78, 79, 82, 85–86, 125, 129, 139
Atlanta Campaign, 65, 85
Atlanta Medical College Hospital, 139

B

Bailey, Mrs. T. B., 126
Baird, Archie, 35
Banks, General N. P., 45, 47
Baptism, 110–11
Barbee, Colonel Joshua, 37, 39
Barbee, Miss Fannie, 38
Barbee, Miss Sallie, 38, 39
Barbee, Mrs., 37
Barthalow, B. A., 128
Battle above the Clouds, xviii, 52, 138
Battlefields of the Civil War, 138
Battles and Leaders of the Civil War, 134
Beauregard, Camp, xiv, 89
Beauregard, General P. G. T., xxiii, 21, 135
Bell, Private J. M., 4
Bell, William Camp, 11
Belmont, battle of, xv, 24–25, 134
Bentonville, battle of, xxiii
Bethel Station, 26
Bible, 81
Bill (Servant), 83
BLA Publishing Ltd., 138
Black, R., 122
Bloomington, 20
Blue and Gray magazine, 136
Blue Ridge Mountains, xxiii
Blythe, Colonel, 107
Bolton, Reverend J. G., 59
Boone, Daniel, 33
Boyle, General Jeremiah T., 40, 137
Bradshaw, S. J., 11

144

SEQUENCE OF LOCATIONS

1. CLOPTON'S CAMP GROUND - NEAR COVINGTON, TN.
2. JACKSON, TN.
3. NEW MADRID, MO.
4. RANDOLPH, TN.
5. HICKMAN, KY.
6. JACKSON, TN.
7. CORINTH, MS.
8. BATTLE OF SHILOH; APRIL 6 & 7, 1862
9. CORINTH, MS.
10. TUPELO, MS.
11. MERIDIAN, MS.
12. MOBILE, AL.
13. MONTGOMERY, AL.
14. ATLANTA, GA.
15. CHATTANOOGA, TN.
16. HARRISON, TN.
17. PERRYVILLE, KY.
18. BATTLE OF PERRYVILLE; OCTOBER 8, 1862
19. KNOXVILLE, TN.
20. WINCHESTER, TN.
21. BATTLE OF MURFREESBORO, TN; DECEMBER 31, 1862 TO JANUARY 2, 1863
22. CHATTANOOGA, TN.
23. BATTLE OF CHICKAMAUGA (GA.) SEPTEMBER 19 & 20, 1863
24. BATTLE OF MISSIONARY RIDGE; NOV. 25, 1863
25. BATTLE OF CAT CREEK
26. ATLANTA, GA.
27. MONTGOMERY, AL.
28. SELMA, AL.
29. DEMOPOLIS, AL.
30. DALTON, GA. (NEAR CHATTANOOGA, TN.)
31. BATTLE OF ROCKY FACE RIDGE (GA)
32. BATTLE OF RESACA, GA; MAY 14 & 15, 1864
33. ACTION AT ADAIRSVILLE, GA.
34. BATTLE OF NEW HOPE CHURCH, GA
35. BATTLE OF DALLAS, GA.
36. BATTLE OF KENNESAW MOUNTAIN, GA; JUNE 27, 1864
37. BATTLE OF PEACHTREE CREEK, GA; JULY 20, 1864
38. BATTLE OF ATLANTA; JULY 22, 1864
39. BATTLE OF JONESBORO, GA.; AUG. 31 - SEPT. 1, 1864
40. BATTLE OF LOVEJOY'S STATION, GA.
41. ACTION AT DALTON, GA.
42. GAYLESVILLE, AL.
43. ACTION AT DECATUR, AL.
44. ACTION AT FLORENCE AL.
45. ACTION AT SPRING HILL, TN.
46. BATTLE OF FRANKLIN, TN.; NOV. 30, 1864
47. BATTLE OF NASHVILLE, TN;
48. ACTION AT SPRING HILL, TN.
49. CORINTH, MS.
50. TUPELO, MS.
51. WEST POINT, MS.
52. MERIDIAN, MS.